LIVING STRENGTH™

ULTIMATE PUSH-UPS

FOR THE AWESOME PHYSIQUE

by Rod Fisher & John e. Peterson

THE LIVING STRENGTH CREED

Strive for excellence in thought, word, and deed.

Acknowledge the Almighty in all that you do.

Love your friends, speak the truth, practice fidelity, and honor your father and mother.

These Godly principles are the foundation of self-mastery. They make you strong of character, give you hope, and guide you on the path to greatness.

–John E. Peterson

The exercises and advice contained within this book may be too strenuous and dangerous for some people, and the reader should consult their health practitioner before engaging in them. The information in this book is for educational purposes only. Neither the publisher nor authors are engaged in rendering professional advice or services to the individual reader. All matters regarding physical and mental health should be supervised by a health practitioner knowledgeable in treating that particular condition. Neither the authors nor the publisher shall be liable or responsible for any loss, injury, or damage allegedly arising from any information or suggestion in this book.

LIVING STRENGTH™
ULTIMATE PUSH-UPS FOR THE AWESOME PHYSIQUE

ISBN 978-0-9894597-0-9

Published by Living Strength Publishing LLC.,
2600 E. 26th Street, Minneapolis, MN 55406

You can reach us on the Internet at **www.LivingStrengthPublishing.com**

Literary development and cover/interior design by
Koechel Peterson & Associates, Inc., Minneapolis, Minnesota

Manufactured in the United States of America

TABLE OF CONTENTS

Preface

If you were to ask me to describe *Ultimate Push-ups for the Awesome Physique* in just one sentence, I'd say, "*Ultimate Push-ups for the Awesome Physique* is the do-it-now, no-excuses, fast-start, get-up-and-go, jump-into-action Bible for super health, awesome strength, off-the-charts fitness, and a chiseled physique for high performance living."

My friend, you have a choice in life. You can sputter and stumble and creak your way along, reading volume after volume of contradictory information about health, exercise, and nutrition, which ultimately only serves to make you frustrated, confused, and apathetic—or you can take charge and transform your health, strength, fitness, and physique, while becoming a human dynamo in the process. The choice is yours.

If you choose to be supercharged, you've come to the right place at the right time, because there is no better way to insure that you will achieve the super health, strength, fitness, and physique of youth that you deserve than by learning the methods and techniques that Rod Fisher and I outline in *Ultimate Push-ups for the Awesome Physique.* We share three customized programs that will totally transform your muscles, reset your mind, recharge your hormones, and give you the kind of unshakable self-confidence that comes from knowing what you can truly do. Best of all, what Rod and I teach requires no equipment—just you, the know-how that we provide, and the time you already have available.

With *Ultimate Push-ups for the Awesome Physique*, the only thing you won't have is an excuse for being in less than perfect shape. Guaranteed.

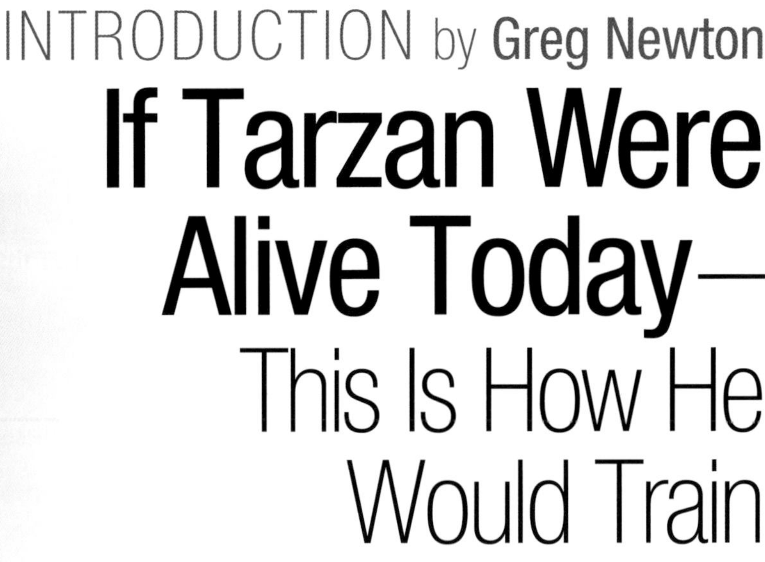

INTRODUCTION by Greg Newton

If Tarzan Were Alive Today—This Is How He Would Train

A bold statement, indeed; this assertion jumped out at me and caught my attention. I was looking at a book—not an ordinary strength training book. This book claimed that you could build a muscular, athletic, and healthy body without weights, machines, gadgets, or drugs.

Having once upon a time owned a fitness center and been a personal trainer, this just did not read right. Yet the pictures in the book were of this confident, smiling guy with a fantastic build, who looked like a cross between a decathlete and a middleweight boxer.

In the book he was demonstrating push-ups, pull-ups, sit-ups, deep knee bends, and self-resistance exercises that looked like the Charles Atlas lessons I did as a kid. *Charles Atlas*? I asked myself. *No way. That muscular tension stuff doesn't work. Or did it?* This guy had a fantastic build and was doing some incredible things. Then I read the kicker. This smiling handsome guy was in his fifties and had never trained with a barbell a day in his life. I was sold.

You see, I was desperately looking for something different in my training. In my mid forties I was washed up as an athlete. For over a decade I had indulged in heavy weight training, thinking this was the Holy Grail of training that was going to keep me fit, strong, and healthy until the end of days. Instead, I was fat, awkward, and inflexible, with no endurance. My joints ached. Sleeping was a chore as I tossed and turned at night trying to get comfortable, because I hurt so badly in my joints and in my spine.

Could I do body weight exercises such as push-ups? Huh, my rotator cuff hurt too bad, and I was winded after the first twenty. How about sit-ups? My back hurt too much, and I was too inflexible to do even one. Pull-ups? Forget it—they weren't happening either. This was the strength and fitness I had to show after a decade of heavy weight training.

You know, the bodybuilding publications never explain that weight training, especially heavy weight training, wears on the joints and the spine. There is always talk of genetics to build muscle, but never that some have better leverages for lifting weights than others, and that if you don't have ideal body proportions for certain lifts, you will wear your body down even more.

If you don't believe me, talk to someone who did heavy lifting or bodybuilding in their twenties and thirties and is still trying to do it in their middle years. What do they look like? Is their gut trim or padded? Is the chest firm or collapsed? Do they look healthy or are they gray in the face?

Ask them about injuries. Do they wake up with pain? Do they have arthritis, and if so, do they have to take medication for it? Ask them if there are any lifts they can't do anymore. What about their back and knees? If they answer honestly, you will be surprised at the answers. I know a guy who contacted me one time to tell me he was lifting weights successfully, and that was after two rotator cuff surgeries! There was definitely a disconnect going on there.

Pushing Yourself to Power by John Peterson was the name of the book. I bought it some years ago now and have never looked back. It opened up a world of fitness to me that strengthened and developed the body in a way that didn't tear down the joints and connective tissue. These exercises actually helped heal old injuries.

However, it gets better than that. The Peterson guy who wrote the book; you know the guy with the fantastic build and the confident smile? He turned out to be a very approachable guy. He invited me to call him one day. Still skeptical, I asked him if training like this actually worked. He laughed and gave me a simple explanation about using the forces of your own body to create muscular contractions without using an external source. He went on to tell me that barbells and machines put extra stress on the tendons and ligaments because of amplified gravity, and that weights compressed the disks of the spine. He encouraged me to try his exercises out for myself and to see if I could feel the difference.

I took his advice. By doing these exercises I lost thirty pounds, recovered strength, became more flexible, and gained endurance to spare. Old wear-and-tear injuries to my knees, shoulders, and back were healed. I also became much more muscular. In my early fifties now, I am actually in better physical condition than when I was a black belt martial artist in my late twenties.

I am also stronger than when I was a heavy weight lifter, which almost seems contradictory. However, whereas I was gym strong before, I now have the strength to climb, run, swim, move my body through space, and lift unwieldy objects in daily tasks. I can actually use my strength for something besides lifting barbells and dumbbells; but should I desire to do so, I can still do that as well.

Recently, to prove that point, I rolled out a 105-pound barbell set and curled it eight times. This was at a body weight of 184 pounds.

My previous best in the curl was 105 for five repetitions over a decade ago and weighing well over 200 pounds with a lifting belt for leverage.

In fact, as far as moving my body weight, I can do hundreds of consecutive deep knee bends, leg raises, and sit-ups; something I had never ever been able to do before. I can also do many more strict push-ups, pull-ups, and chin-ups than I have ever done in my entire life. Push-ups in particular have driven the train, and I now routinely do 500 or more a day, along with the various tension and self-resistance exercises that John Peterson teaches.

How about the "overuse" injuries you supposedly get from doing hundreds of repetitions of calisthenics every day? If you train as John recommends, with safe form and moderate intensity, you'll find that movements natural to the body don't cause wear and tear.

Training Tarzan style definitely has its advantages. It definitely has enhanced the overall quality of my life. How about that John Peterson fellow who wrote the book? Is he some busted-up athlete, now resting on his laurels?

Not hardly. At sixty years of age, he still has that fantastic build and is doing things the majority of athletes only dream of. How many guys do you know of any age who can knock out thirty or more pull-ups at a moment's notice, run a 10K. or sport a 29" waist? So yes, if Tarzan were an actual real person and alive today, his name would have to be John Peterson.

Greg Newton

chapter ONE

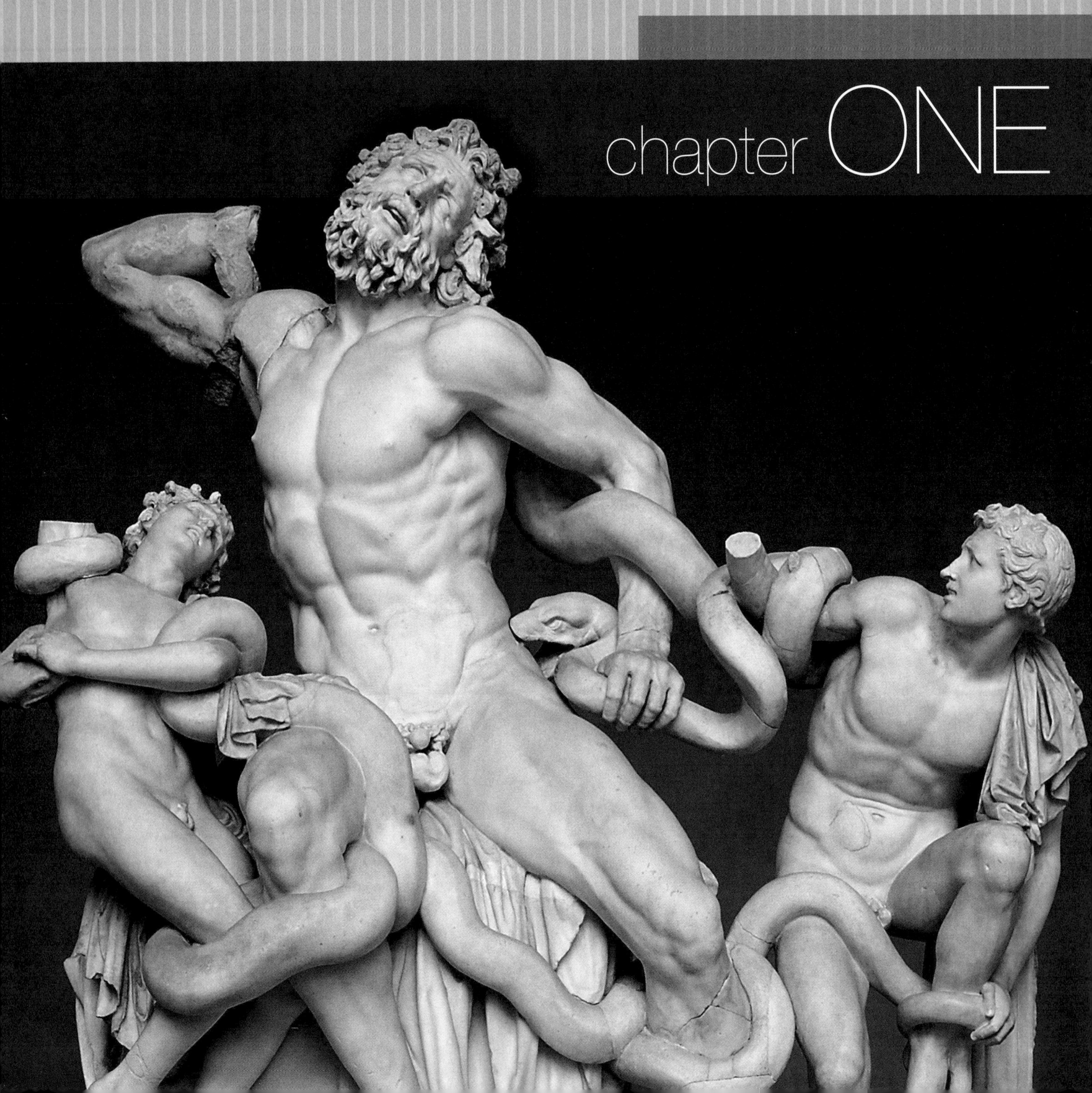

mastery

STEP ONE
Self-Mastery

"Do not believe in anything simply because you have heard it. Do not believe in anything simply because it is spoken and rumored by many. Do not believe in anything simply because it is found written in your religious books. Do not believe in anything merely on the authority of your teachers and elders. Do not believe in traditions because they have been handed down for many generations. But after observation and analysis, when you find that anything agrees with reason and is conducive to the good and benefit of one and all, then accept it and live up to it."

PRINCE SIDDHARTHA GAUTAMA

STEP ONE
Self-Mastery

Your success with *Living Strength Ultimate Push-ups for the Awesome Physique* (Course #1 of the Living Strength Total Health System for Super Health, Strength, Fitness, and Healing) will be predicated on your willingness to follow the instructions presented in this chapter to the letter. Failure to carry out *all* of the instructions or entertaining the misguided notion that this chapter is unnecessary fluff, filler, or perhaps "beneath you" is a sure sign of arrogance on your part and proof positive that you are totally unaware of the single most important exercise in existence—*programming the right thoughts into your mind for total self-mastery*. As a consequence, you will be standing in your own way and preventing yourself from achieving the ultimate success you could otherwise have.

So let's be honest with each other from the start. You would not have invested in this course if you were not influenced by the thoughts you were consciously thinking at the time you purchased it. Likewise, you will not take the necessary action to give yourself the supreme levels of health, strength, fitness, and physique that you deserve, unless you begin with the exact outcome you want to accomplish clearly defined in your mind. If you try to prove me wrong on this point, you will only be shortchanging yourself and sabotaging your own success.

Here's the point I want to drive home. So many people think that fitness success and achieving a beautifully sculpted body is nothing more than knowing the right exercises to do and eating the right foods. Although both are critically important and part of the long-term answer, the truth is you cannot get the results you want, much less adhere to the right exercise and nutritional program, *unless your mind is properly programmed first. No exceptions. Your mind-set will determine your outcome.*

Take a look around, my friend. There are hundreds of thousands of people who pay expensive gym memberships, purchase expensive training programs from infomercials they see promoted on television and the Internet, exercise and diet year after year, take stimulants and drugs, and yet they are still overweight and totally lacking in the muscle definition they want. They go through the motions, but the only thing getting thinner is their wallet. *Why is that?* It's because they don't understand the life-changing power that God has placed within them. Even worse, when introduced to it, some flat out reject it. They are literally afraid to take control of their own thinking mechanism. Truth to tell, these people fear that any attempt to harness their mind will

John Peterson, *age 60,* performs push-ups and Isometrics daily with the Isometric Power Belt.

backfire. Instead of boldly living the life of their dreams, they timidly settle for whatever life hands them. In other words, they want someone else to do their thinking and give them the answers, and that, my friend, is not only sad, it's living by default and placing one's self in a position of perpetual victimhood and helpless enslavement. In such a state, the only way life can improve for such people is if the person to whom they have given their power and right to self-determination chooses to make life better for them. Can you think of anything sadder or more pathetic than someone who deliberately chooses the role of being enslaved and victimized by others? Unfortunately, it happens every day, and we now live in a society that reinforces such victimhood.

However, living by default and dependence on someone else is not the way to achieve personal transformation and magnetic personal power. And it certainly has no part in achieving true Living Strength. Realize that your future success will be because *you* have made the right choices in order to make it possible. Why is that the case? Because you have learned that you can trust yourself. You, and you alone, decide what you want to accomplish in life—and you will make up your mind *now* that whatever it takes and no matter what sacrifice is required, you *will* do it to achieve your desired goal.

First Things First

The *Golden Key* to making the life-changing transition to a consciousness that attracts a wonderful level of success and repels failure is not difficult to learn. And it does not require a lot of time. It only requires dedication and persistence. Just follow the step-by-step procedures outlined in this chapter, and you will be on your way to the success you desire in no time flat.

Begin With Deep Costal Breathing

Why deep costal breathing?

1. Breath is L-I-F-E, and therefore Breath is P-O-W-E-R.

2. Deep costal (chest) breathing calms the central nervous system (CNS) and centers the mind, allowing you to focus your thoughts in much the same way as a laser beam.

3. Deep costal breathing creates a heightened state of awareness in which you realize that you can create whatever you want in life.

Consider the creation story in the Holy Bible as found in the first chapters of Genesis. There you will find some fascinating insights into the process of creation. First of all, it is very clear that whenever God created something, He first pictured it in His mind and then literally spoke it into existence. Also note that when God created the first man, Adam, he did not come to life until God breathed life into him. This is exactly what the text says in Genesis 2:7: *"the Lord God formed man from the dust of the ground and breathed into his nostrils the breath of life, and man became a living being."* (Can you imagine what Adam must have looked like with the Lord God as his sculptor?)

I relate this creation story for one reason—because the *Golden Key* to making miracles happen in your life begins the exact same way. You establish order and clarity by first calming the mind and picturing in vivid detail what it is that you want. *Then you add the life, power, vitality, and energy to this mental image by breathing life into it.*

The good news is that this process is not difficult to learn.

Not only that, but the deep costal breathing method I am about to teach you will simultaneously accomplish a number of positive things that will enhance your life immeasurably. Before I tell you what they are, let's learn the exercise.

Here Is What to Do:

In the morning, as soon as you awake and *before arising,* relax your entire body with your hands at your sides.

1. Lie on your back and relax your body.

2. Place your left hand (palm down) on your sternum and right hand (palm down) on your abdomen.

3. Inhale deeply (through your nostrils on the inhalation) and fill your entire body with life-sustaining oxygen. Visualize that your body is one giant lung (or balloon)—then imagine pulling the inhalation all the way from your feet. At first the hand on your abdomen will naturally lift as your lower lungs fill. As you continue to inhale you will feel your chest expand and visably rise as your abdomen is drawn in. When your lungs are filled to maximum capacity, the clavicles (collarbones) lift.

4. Once you have inhaled to the maximum, hold for a few seconds and then slowly begin to exhale through your mouth.

5. During the exhalation, flex, squeeze, and pull in your abdominal muscles as though you were wringing water from a towel. Tighten and squeeze them from the bottom to the top and feel as though you are trying to draw in the front of your abdomen to touch your spine.

6. As you squeeze during the exhalation, make an *s-s-s-s* sound through your teeth that literally sounds like air being let out of a tire, and continue making this sound until your exhalation is completely finished. Leave nothing in your lungs.

7. While exhaling and squeezing your abdominal muscles, it is also a healthy practice

to contract and pull in your perineum (this can only be done if you are pulling the abdomen in). This will not only enhance your overall energy, but it will also increase and concentrate your sexual power and energy.

8. Perform this deep costal breathing exercise 12 times (2 minutes tops—6 breaths a minute) in succession before getting out of bed. Next, continue to do 12 more of the same exercise while standing before an open window (assuming that it is not freezing). To do this, stand upright with shoulders back and chest forward. Really see and feel your chest expand and rise to the utmost on each breath as your abdomen is drawn in. This is "costal breathing" as was taught by master Physical Culturist Edwin Checkley, and it was the basis and foundation of Edwin Checkley's own Physical Culture Training System that mirrors our own. We also recommend that you perform this exercise many times throughout the entire day, especially before you perform any physical exertion and also to instantly "recharge and energize" and rid yourself of mental fatigue or stress.

Now that you have read the instructions, take just a few minutes and practice this deep costal breathing technique 12 times. In order to motivate you even more, and just in case you missed the incredible benefits outlined in the steps above, here are just some of the benefits you will derive from this type of breathing:

- Enhanced sense of calm, clarity, and mental alertness.
- Enhanced creativity and mental focus.
- Eliminates and rids the body and mind of negative stress.
- Immediately increases vitality, energy, and muscular strength.
- Tightens, sculpts, and strengthens the abdominal muscles.
- Improves digestion, assimilation, and elimination.
- Purifies the lungs of stale residue while enhancing and expanding lung capacity.
- Helps you to relax and release nervous energy.
- Enhances overall body power due to strengthening of the core muscles.
- Enhances stamina and sexual function.

Enough said. If you performed the 12 repetitions, you will actually feel the life-enhancing power of this breathing technique. Once you have finished your set of 12 deep costal breaths, you should literally feel that you moved into a different state of physical and intellectual vibration. Put simply, you should feel a sense of power and clarity and, generally speaking, you should glow and feel *good* all over.

It is this *good* feeling that is the *Golden Key* to success in life, especially when you know how to harness and combine it with the other mental programming techniques that you are about to learn *N-O-W*.

We often hear it said, "We become what we think about," but the bottom line is that it is only partially true. We don't just automatically become what we think about as the sages have said. Rather, we become what we think about only when we add deep emotion, unshakable conviction, and a laser-like focus to that specific thought and its desired outcome *again and again*. To merely think a thought, especially about something that you believe is out of your reach, which is often referred to as "wishful thinking," does not give it the power to be transformed into anything . . . let alone reality.

But to *think, believe,* and *know* that any given thought and its achievement are totally within our grasp are the key. W. Clement Stone so eloquently stated this in his often quoted statement: *"Whatever the mind of man can conceive and believe, it can achieve."* And then to think and focus on that thought again and again and to back it with an abundance of enthusiasm, positive action, and emotion has the power to transform that thought into reality. It's literally what Henry David Thoreau was referring to when he stated, *"As a single footstep will not make a path on the earth, so a single thought will not make a pathway in the mind. To make a deep physical path, we walk again and again. To make a deep mental path, we must think over and over the kind of thoughts we wish to dominate our lives."*

Understand that each of us thinks in pictures. This understanding is crucial to giving you the mental tools and mind-set that you need to achieve whatever aims you have. Let's consider a few examples. Think of your home. What comes to mind? A picture, right? Think of your mom and dad; your best friend; your car; your wardrobe; your favorite movie; your favorite restaurant; your favorite vacation place; your first kiss. What came to mind? One picture, followed by another, and another, continuing through the entire list, correct?

Now that you understand this, it's time to form a mental picture of the kind of physique you want to have. Do you want to add a lot of size and muscle mass? Or do you want to slim down and get ultra lean and ripped? Either desire can be achieved with *Living Strength Ultimate Push-ups for the Awesome Physique,* and you will see the visual proof in the many men featured throughout the pages that follow.

Consider this important and essential point. Some people erroneously believe that you add muscle mass only as the result of intense exercise itself. You don't. For instance, my friend Jack King who is a former champion Olympic style weightlifter would tell you there are Olympic weightlifters who practice all of the Olympic lifts with very heavy weights but never gain an ounce of body weight because they want to remain within their given weight class. It's done all the time. The same is also true of Olympic wrestlers and boxers. These men train with great intensity at all times, yet they remain within their respective weight classes.

So what then is the key to either gaining muscle mass or losing body fat with any given exercise program? Answer: *your intention.* Seriously, what exactly is it that you want to accomplish? Tell your muscles how you want them to respond to the exercises, and they will obey.

You see, your flesh has an intelligence of its own, and it simply sits back and waits for you to give it marching orders through vivid and clear direction. Once the orders are clearly given, every cell in your body will go to work to comply with your orders and shape your body the way you have directed it.

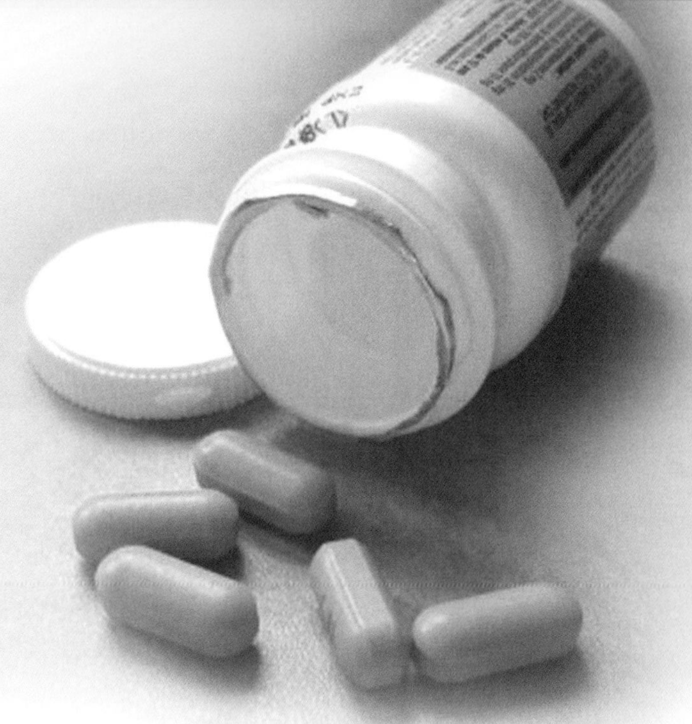

For instance, we have all read stories of people who have had life-threatening illnesses and have had remarkable recoveries and made themselves well by taking control of the thoughts they think. My friend Jack King is a perfect example, as you will discover when you read his bio in chapter 2. And we also know that perfectly healthy people can make themselves sick by thinking negatively. Want further proof? Consider the following true story that I first shared in my book *Pushing Yourself to Power.*

The Extraordinary Case of Mr. Wright

In an article published in 1957 by psychologist Bruno Klopfer in *The Journal of Prospective Techniques,* entitled "Psychological Variables in Human Cancer," a man called Mr. Wright suffered from advanced lymphatic cancer. Orange-sized tumors had invaded his neck, groin, chest, and abdomen; both his spleen and liver were so enlarged that two quarts of milky fluid had to be drained from them daily. The doctors had done everything medically possible in the mid 1950s on Mr. Wright's behalf, but there was nothing more they could do. So they gave him up to die.

Somehow Mr. Wright heard of a new experimental drug for cancer called *Krebiozen.* But it was only being administered to people whom doctors believed had at least a three-month life expectancy. Wright begged his doctor for the drug, and finally the doctor relented. According to the report, the doctor injected him on Friday but really didn't expect him to live through the weekend.

Mr. Wright was bedridden and fighting for each breath when he received his first injection of *Krebiozen*. But three days later he was cheerfully ambling around the unit, joking with the nurses. Mr. Wright's tumors had shrunk by half, and after ten more days of treatment he was discharged from the hospital, having been acknowledged by the doctors to be *cancer free!*

Unfortunately, months later the American Medical Association published a nationwide study on *Krebiozen* that flatly announced it was worthless. Mr. Wright read the study, believed it, and his cancer returned. Two days later he died.

So what happened to Mr. Wright? Why did he become wrong? Let's examine it objectively. Mr. Wright, who is terminal, hears about a new miracle cure for cancer. He thinks to himself that the reason he has not already died is because it is his destiny to be cured of cancer, and *Krebiozen* is the agent of that cure. He begs his doctor to go outside the rule and inject him. Then Mr. Wright's mind and emotions *believe* that the miraculous cure has been found, and as a result his body obeys the single congruent message that it is given by Mr. Wright's own mind, which is—HEAL! And his body has no other choice but to obey!

Just think what would have happened had Mr. Wright not read the study that negated his positive belief. Who knows how long he could have lived? But the simple point is this: Whatever you believe about yourself, both intellectually and emotionally, will determine who and what you become physically and spiritually. For that reason alone you must guard your thoughts, your speech, and all of your associations. If you surround yourself with positive reinforcement in what you see, hear, think, and verbalize, and if you follow through with positive action—you will meet with a positive outcome. It is inevitable! In fact, it is for this reason that you must never allow yourself to think or verbalize anything about yourself that you do not wish to be completely true.

So why did I share this story with you? What's the point? It's because I want you to realize that the vast majority of people miss the boat completely and do not realize the power that harnessing their thoughts has as it applies to their state of strength, fitness, and physique. But it does!

Take for instance my close friend Greg Newton, whom you have already met and seen in the introduction of this book. Greg uses the same exercises that I follow. Yet by his own admission, he used them differently when he first began and went from a body weight of 215 pounds down to a lithe, athletic, and muscular 185 pounds. How did he do this? Well, first and foremost, by *wanting* to do so. Next, he thought about his goal with great conviction throughout the day. And third, he held the image he wanted to achieve in his mind's eye and positively reinforced it *while he trained.* It's as simple as that.

The unrevealed "secret" that everyone wants to know, the secret that the vast majority of people do not know, is not just picturing what you want—but picturing it with great conviction and backing that conviction with positive action. It also means that you must refuse all contradictory programming from outside sources that are negative. By carefully controlling what goes into your mind and putting white-hot action behind your desire, you cannot help but go in the direction you want. This is a Universal Law that was eloquently expressed by Henry David Thoreau in his classic *Walden*: *"I learned this, that if one advances confidently in the direction of his dreams, and endeavors to live the life which he has imagined, he will meet with a success unexpected in common hours. He will put some things behind, will pass an invisible boundary; new, universal, and more liberal laws will begin to establish themselves around and within him; or the old laws be expanded, and interpreted in his favor in a more liberal sense, and he will live with the license of a higher order of beings."*

Now, how do you go about adding positive emotion and great conviction to achieve your goal? Pay attention. You start by inhaling deeply and feeling your chest expand to the maximum while energizing your entire being, *visualize* your desired outcome by forming a mental picture of exactly what it is that you desire, and then quite literally surround that mental image (your desired goal) with breath. This time instead of focusing on contracting and squeezing your abdominal muscles through the formation of a mental picture and internalized verbal command (self-talk) as is done in the standard deep breathing exercise, you will now squeeze (adding conviction and emotion) to the goal (mental image) you have visualized. Next, after you have completed your inhalation, begin your exhalation. Once again surround the goal you have visualized with this same energy. Literally exhale into the image you have visualized, surrounding it with power. This is how it is done.

Understand that there is a reason why all champion athletes begin their performance with deep breathing while in a deep meditative state. The same thing can and should be done before any creative endeavor is attempted. Whether it includes painting, drawing, sculpting, writing, or singing, you start with deep costal breathing.

Now, let's consider the biblical creation story as told in the book of Genesis again. In Genesis 2:7, it states, "*Then the LORD God formed the man out of the dust from the ground and breathed the breath of life into his nostrils, and the man became a living being.*" God breathed life into Adam. Whether you personally believe the biblical account as I do is NOT my point. My point is that the procedure described in the book of Genesis is exactly what you want to use in your own life. Always remember that you are not just a MAN (or WOMAN) but a human being created in the image of God with the same creative God-like ability to create that is described in the book of Genesis. After all, since it states that man is made in the image and likeness of God—and God is the Creator—doesn't it make sense that man, too, was intended to be a creator—and is happiest and most God-like when he is involved in actively creating.

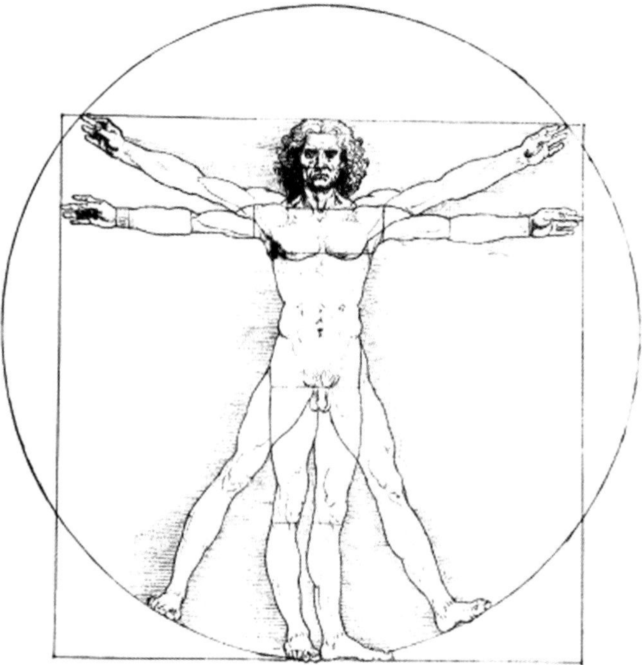

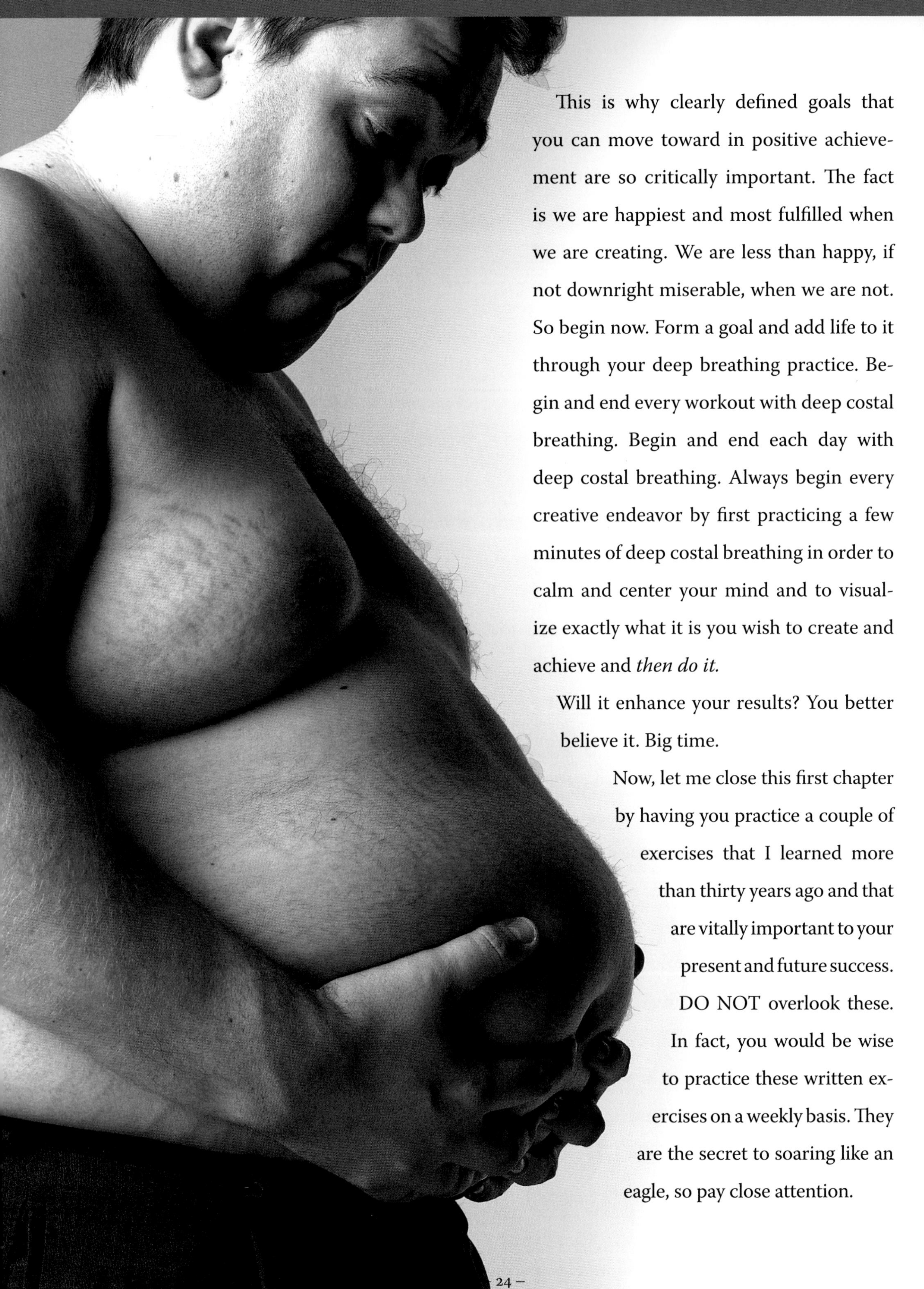

This is why clearly defined goals that you can move toward in positive achievement are so critically important. The fact is we are happiest and most fulfilled when we are creating. We are less than happy, if not downright miserable, when we are not. So begin now. Form a goal and add life to it through your deep breathing practice. Begin and end every workout with deep costal breathing. Begin and end each day with deep costal breathing. Always begin every creative endeavor by first practicing a few minutes of deep costal breathing in order to calm and center your mind and to visualize exactly what it is you wish to create and achieve and *then do it.*

Will it enhance your results? You better believe it. Big time.

Now, let me close this first chapter by having you practice a couple of exercises that I learned more than thirty years ago and that are vitally important to your present and future success. DO NOT overlook these. In fact, you would be wise to practice these written exercises on a weekly basis. They are the secret to soaring like an eagle, so pay close attention.

Many people, in fact the vast majority of people, when asked to define what it is they want in life, literally draw a blank. They cannot think clearly about what they want in life because their mind has already been totally preoccupied with what they DON'T want for so long that it appears as though nothing else is possible for them.

Never forget that we become what we habitually think about with deep conviction and emotion. And so, if you can't even think and clearly define what it is YOU WANT because you have invested all of your thought capital into what you don't want—guess what you have created and are continuing to create? Three guesses, and two don't count. That's right. More of what you do not want.

Well, my friend, it's time you gave yourself the break you deserve. Unbeknownst to you, that may be exactly why you picked up this book. It's time you leave your self-created, self-limiting hell once and for all. So let me show you how. You're going to start by making two lists. One list will be everything you want to achieve and experience in your life. The other list is a list of what you don't want—the list you will write first.

So, before doing anything else, take out a pen and get a piece of notebook paper (with lines if possible) and get ready to fill out the page with . . .

Things **I Don't Want** to Have, Do, or Experience **in My Life**

Things I Don't Want to Have, Do, or Experience in My Life

Now, beneath this headline start writing them down and leave nothing out. List everything that comes to mind regardless of how painful it may be at the moment. Part of healing your life and moving forward to a life of blessing is to have the guts to face what you don't want and to not hide from it. If you have the guts to face it, you'll have the guts to eradicate it from your life once and for all. For example...

- I don't want to be fat and out of shape.
- I don't want to feel weak and inferior to other men.
- I don't want any more back pain or pain in my joints.
- I don't want to be taking meds that I would not need if I were in super shape.
- I don't want these headaches.
- I don't want to wear clothes that look like they were made for an elephant.
- I don't want to be afraid to work out in public in a tank top and shorts.
- I don't want to ever be ashamed of my appearance.
- I don't want to be afraid to ask women to go out with me.

You get the picture, so now just do it. Start by moving your pen across the paper and write whatever comes to mind. DO IT NOW!

Seriously. Do it. It's your key to a brighter and better future. So don't move until you have done this exercise. Put your pen on the paper and fill it out with all the things you don't want to do, have, or experience and that you want to completely eliminate from your life. If you need more motivation, consider this quote from my good friend Dr. Chuck Missler and write it down: *"Tomorrow is the day that idle men work and fools repent."* Bottom line: Get to work and do it now! Come back as soon as you finish.

Got it done? Great! After you're done writing the list of the things you don't want, your mind will be focused like a laser. That means that you are now ready to make the list of all the good things that you truly want and desire that will be of benefit to you and every other person in your life. However, before we write that list there is one thing we must do. We need to take the list of the negative things that we do not want in our lives and take it to a sink or bathtub or anywhere that is totally safe and burn it! Seriously, burning the list of the negative and hurtful things that you do not want in your life sends a powerful message to your subconscious mind that reinforces your decision to be free of those negative things once and for all. It literally symbolizes burning the bridge behind you. So do it now.

The Good Things You Truly Want

Now we can address the good stuff. One thing you should be aware of is that you can and should feel free to write down *anything* you truly want to achieve that is for the benefit of one and all. It does not have to all be totally related to strength and fitness, though I would think that at least a few items listed should be related to health, strength, and fitness, since that is the subject we are focusing on in this course of exercise. Nonetheless, feel free to include spiritual goals, intellectual goals, relationship goals, financial goals, and any other positive and beneficial goals that you can think or imagine. And please remember that it is not necessary for anyone else to lose in life in order for you to win.

So this is what you do. Take a new sheet of paper and write the following headline at the top of the page, **The Top 10 Most Important Things I Want to Create in My Life—Within the Next 12 Months.** For example, your list might be something like this:

- I want to weigh 180 pounds and have a 30" waistline and a 46" chest.
- I want to fit into the jeans I wore 5 years ago.
- I want to be able to do 5 sets of 50 consecutive Living Strength Push-ups, Sit-ups, and Squats.
- I want to be able to do 20 Full Range Pull-ups in good form.
- I want to attract the perfect mate into my life.
- I want to move into a new home.
- I want to double my current income.
- I want to read the entire Bible in one year.
- I want to double my charitable giving.
- I want to help others become healthy, strong, and happy.
- I want to be a good role model for my sons.

Got the idea? Great! Take the next few minutes and write down the top 10 goals that you want to achieve in the next 12 months. If it is far more than 10 items on your list, that's fine, but make sure that it is at least 10. Do it NOW!

Good job! Now that you have your top 10 goals written out, you can always go back to them in order to refine them and flesh out the details. In fact, the more complete and vivid the details become, the quicker and more powerful the result. The *Golden Key,* however, is to identify them and write them down, because this takes them from the realm of thought and puts them into the realm of substance.

One Major Goal

The next thing to do after you have made up your list is to select one specific goal that you will focus on achieving over the next 28 days. This is what I refer to as the *dynamic breakthrough technique.* It is a supreme confidence builder. This is how it is done: Choose something from your list that you can accomplish within 28 days or even as little as 7 days. If you don't have a short-term goal on your list, take just a few minutes now to come up with one. For example: *In the next 28 days I will perform 50 push-ups in perfect form.*

The purpose of having a specific short-term goal is to build unshakable confidence as quickly as possible. You see, once you know that you can focus on a specific goal like a laser beam and make it happen, your creative power and your nerve force literally surge to new heights. This then makes it possible to tackle bigger and bigger goals at a much faster clip.

Once you have selected that one specific goal, you will now focus on its completion. This is best accomplished by writing the selected goal on a 3" x 5" goal card. For example, let's say that today is March 1 and that presently you can perform 24 push-ups in good form. Let's also say that your goal is to complete 50 push-ups in perfect form within the next 28 days. You might write something like the following on your goal card: *Today is March 1. In exactly 28 days, on March 28, I will perform 50 push-ups in perfect form.*

You get the idea. But take special note: The point is to write something that is realistic, totally measurable, completely achievable, and yet has a specific deadline for its achievement. Goals without deadlines have no power to them and are nothing more than wishes.

Now, each morning focus on your one goal when you get up. Find a mirror. Look yourself in the eye and while practicing deep costal breathing read your goal card out loud with deep conviction in your voice. Repeat it a dozen times along with your dozen breaths. Picture yourself in your mind's eye as having already achieved it. And while you picture it, add the breath of life into that image. Feel the sense of satisfaction that comes from positive achievement.

Carry your goal card everywhere you go. Keep it in your front pants pocket or in your wallet. Take it out at least a half-dozen times throughout the day and read it with deep conviction (out loud if possible). *This is especially important to do both before and after each set of push-ups that you perform while practicing deep costal breathing.* By doing so you will increase your level of focus and train much harder as a result.

Most important, notice how fast you improve.

While you train, use positive self-talk. Literally say, "I can. I am. I will." Then repeat it in context. "I can and will do 50 push-ups in perfect form by March 28."

What I have just given you is the MASTER KEY to goal achievement in any area of your life. This is a technique that has been employed and taught by master motivational speaker Brian Tracy for decades. In fact, Mr. Tracy presents validated research in his seminars substantiating the fact that written goals with specific deadlines are the master key to mega-performance breakthroughs in any endeavor. Without written and specific goals, you can achieve very little by comparison.

This first chapter is the most important of all. Why? Because there are hundreds if not thousands of good, well-written books that can teach you how to exercise and put you on a diet and tell you what to do. But what I have just done is to put the power in your hands that ties it all together and makes it work! In other words, the whole key to creating the wonderful and positive changes you want to experience in your life lies inside of you, and now you know how to access it. So, DO IT!

Let's now move to chapter 2 where I will provide you with some inspiring role models.

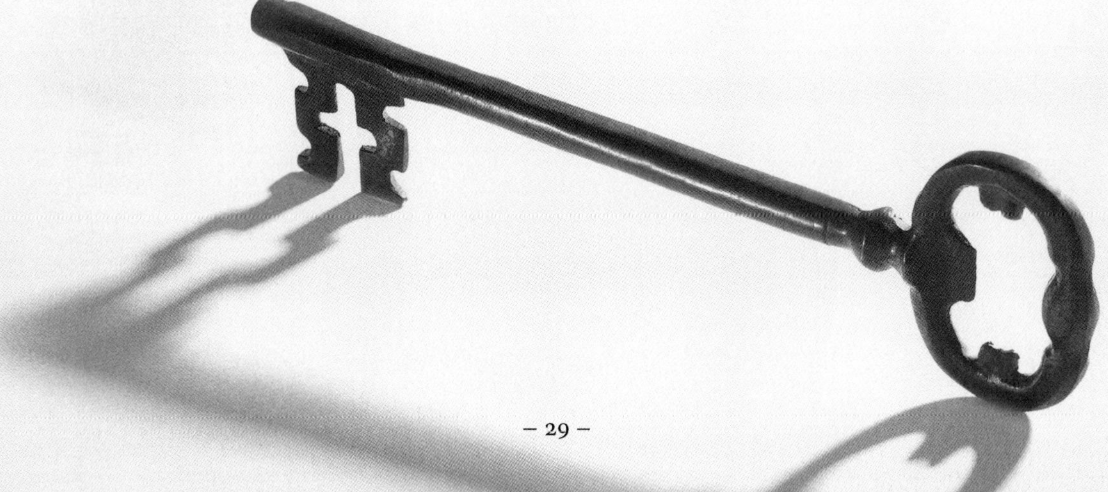

"There is a principle which is a bar against all information, which is proof against all arguments and which cannot fail to keep a man in everlasting ignorance—that principle is condemnation prior to investigation."

Noel Johnson

chapter TWO

the Proof

"THOSE WHO SAY SOMETHING CANNOT BE DONE SHOULD NOT INTERRUPT THOSE WHO ARE DOING IT." —GEORGE BERNARD SHAW

With the above statement in mind, I want to introduce you to five men who have done it. Each of the men you are about to meet developed an extraordinary level of natural strength, fitness, and physique using exactly the same methods you are about to learn in the pages that follow. The truth is that you have always had everything you have ever needed in order to achieve an extraordinary level of superior health, awesome strength, high-level functional fitness, and a beautifully sculpted physique. In fact, it's something that God blessed you with the day you were born. That something is your own magnificent body. Let me prove it to you in the pages that follow.

Charles Atlas

THE WORLD'S MOST PERFECTLY DEVELOPED MAN

In a very real sense, the history of the push-up as the Master bodybuilding exercise of all time would be totally incomplete and lacking without mention of "The World's Most Perfectly Developed Man," Charles Atlas. It would be like telling the history of the D-Day invasion of Normandy, France, on June 6, 1944, without the mention of General Dwight D. Eisenhower, the Supreme Commander of the Allied Forces during World War II. After all, when it comes to the push-up, no one did more to popularize this one superior bodybuilding exercise than the legendary Charles Atlas.

So here goes. Charles Atlas was born in Acri, Italy, on October 30, 1893, with the birth name of Angelo Siciliano. He emigrated to the United States with his mother when he was ten years old. During his early teens, he was often victimized by an older bully in a manner nearly identical to the character

"Mac" in the famous Charles Atlas cartoon ads—"The Insult That Made a Man Out of Mac"—that were so popular in the comic books of the 1930s–1970s. "Mac" was the scrawny guy with the beautiful girl at the beach, and the big bruiser of a bully kicks sand in his face and then threatens to smash in Mac's face. Feeling totally humiliated, Mac sees a "Charles Atlas Dynamic Tension" ad in a magazine and promptly writes to Charles Atlas. Within a relatively short period of time, Mac the Scrawny becomes Mac the Mighty, and he looks in the mirror and says, "It didn't take Charles Atlas long to give me these muscles." He then goes back to the same beach, sees the same bozo who had earlier embarrassed him now humiliating someone else, and promptly dispatches the idiot with a thunderous right cross and hands the guy's butt to him. Of course, the girl is thrilled and says, "Oh, Mac, you are a real man after all." And there are several other onlookers making statements such as "Wow! Look at that guy's build" and "He's already famous for it."

The truth is that that whole cartoon episode really happened to young Angelo Siciliano. But at the time, young Angelo didn't have Charles Atlas to write to because Charles Atlas did not yet exist. So instead he did the next best thing: He wrote to Alois P. Swoboda. And it was the Swoboda Method, an all-natural system of strength and physique development without the use of equipment and strong emphasis on the push-up, that put young Angelo on the fast track to physical transformation and perfection. So much so that one day when Angelo was on the beach with his friends, one of them said, "Hey, Charley [Angelo's nickname], you're looking just like that Atlas guy in the statue." As soon as his friend said it, something clicked and it wasn't long before young Angelo Siciliano legally changed his name to Charles Atlas and became the stuff of legend.

With his newly sculpted physique, Charles Atlas became a highly paid model, posing for many famous sculptors of the day. He also worked at a sideshow on Coney Island, performing as a strongman, and even toured the vaudeville circuit with his friend Earle Liederman in a hand-balancing act. Then in 1921, he won the title of "The World's Most Perfectly Developed Man" in a contest sponsored by Bernarr MacFadden and *Physical Culture* magazine. When Atlas won the title again in 1922, MacFadden gave up sponsoring it, saying, "What's the use? Atlas would win it every time."

Atlas then teamed up with Dr. Fredrich Tilney, a noted health writer and physical

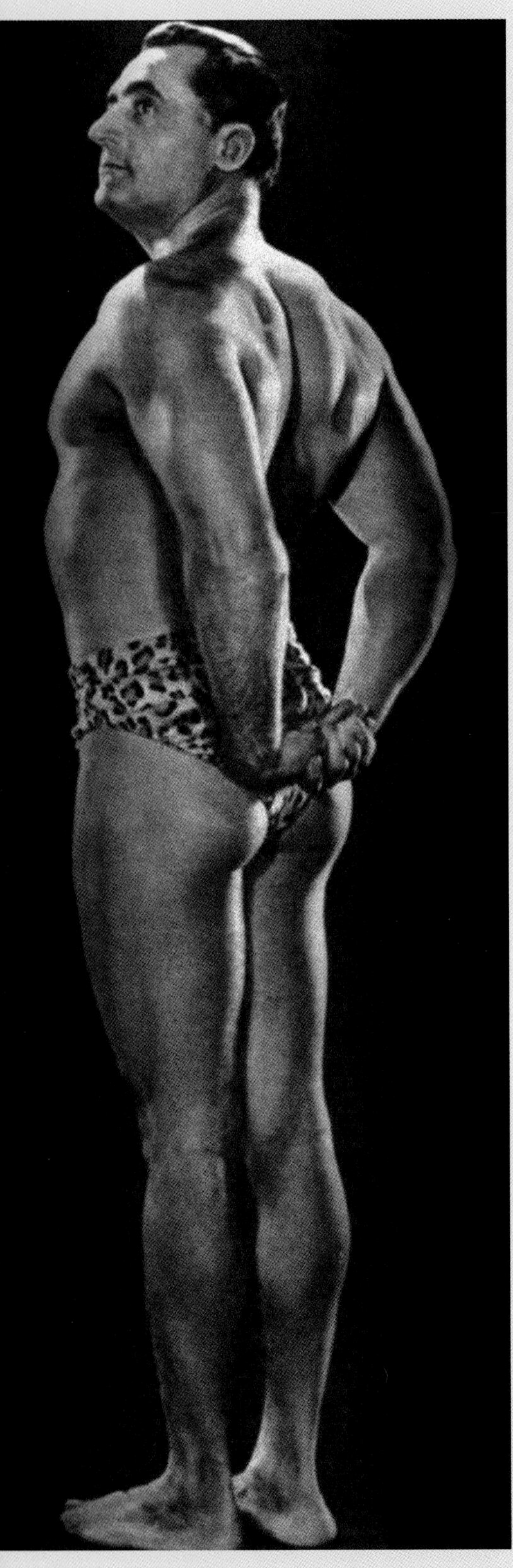

culturist, and published the world famous Charles Atlas Exercise Course in 1922. Initially, the Atlas course was advertised and promoted primarily in *Physical Culture* magazine and was only moderately successful. But in 1929, Charles Atlas was joined by a young, enterprising advertising executive by the name of Charles Roman, and they were off to the races. The first thing Roman did was to change the name of the course as well as coin, copyright, and trademark the term for the exercise methods that were featured in the course—"Dynamic Tension." He also rewrote the ads and promotional material so that they appealed as much to teenage boys as to grown men. Hence, there were multiple variations of the ad, "The Insult That Made a Man Out of Mac." Roman ran these ads in comic books, realizing there was an ever-growing army of teens who wanted to become strong and manly like Charles Atlas. In addition, Roman set up numerous feats of strength for Atlas to perform in public in order to create even more publicity. In fact, throughout the 1930s–1950s, Atlas was never out of the public eye. The team of Altas and Roman was so successful that both men became millionaires *during* the Great Depression of the 1930s.

It can even further be stated that the Atlas Dynamic Tension Method became the stuff of legend in another way. On February 15, 1933, the superhero "Doc Savage, the Man of Bronze" was introduced in magazine form to an anxious and ever-growing American teen market. (In fact, Lester Dent, who wrote the Doc Savage novels under the pseudonym of Kenneth Robeson, said that his target audience was fifteen-year-old boys who wanted to become like the superhero Clark "Doc" Savage.) Beginning with the very first issue, Dent made it clear that "Doc" developed his incredible strength and musculature by performing Charles Atlas's Dynamic Tension exercises for two hours every day. And unlike other writers of the day, Lester Dent did not have a weakness for wine, women, and song. According to his wife, when Lester wrote the Savage novels, he was drinking quarts of milk and practicing Dynamic Tension just like the superhero of his novels! That is the type of advertising that money can't buy.

In addition, there were world famous athletes and celebrities of all types who used the Charles Atlas Dynamic Tension exercises. Heavyweight boxing champions Max Baer, Joe Louis, and Rocky Marciano, baseball players such as Joe DiMaggio and Ted Williams, and even Robert Ripley proudly stated that he was an Atlas student ("believe it or not"). There was Mahatma Gandhi in far-off India and members of the royal family in Britain, and a future U.S. president who wrote to Charles Atlas in 1942 in order to become strong enough to pass the enlistment standards for the U.S. Navy. Similar to hundreds of thousands of other young men, John F. Kennedy turned to Charles Atlas in order to get into top physical form and fulfill his patriotic duty by enlisting for World War II, and in the process became a war hero.

After the war, Charles Atlas was a frequent guest on radio programs, and then as television became a media sensation, a whole new generation of America's teenagers was introduced to Charles Atlas and his method of Dynamic Tension. In fact, Mr. Atlas remained popular right up until his death in the early 1970s, and his Dynamic Tension Training System is still being sold today by Charles Atlas Limited.

So what exactly is the Charles Atlas Dynamic Tension Method? Simply put, it is a series of dynamic self-resistance exercises for every muscle group in the body. In all, there are more than ninety exercises. These are then combined with a selection of power calisthenic exercises of which the Atlas Push-up between chairs is listed first and foremost and is literally the foundation of the entire Charles Atlas Training System, and that point is driven home in lesson one as well as several subsequent lessons.

One other interesting piece of information about Charles Atlas and his methods was published in the April 17, 1964, edition of *Life* magazine. The title was: "Atlas Was Right All Along."

Jock Mahoney

STRENGTH AND FITNESS TARZAN STYLE

As a ten-year-old kid, one of my favorite summertime activities was fishing on Lake Pepin with my grandpa and Uncle Wally. And such was the case on one Saturday in late July 1963. We had been fishing on Lake Pepin since shortly before sunup, and we were having a great time. But just before noon, rather suddenly, the sky turned pitch black, and the wind and waves started kicking up big time. As you might expect, we had to make tracks and get off Lake Pepin as fast as possible.

On the way in to the boat launch, my grandpa said, "How would you boys like to see the Tarzan movie over at the Wabasha Theater this afternoon?" Needless to say, it didn't require much to convince two ten-year-olds and two twelve-year-olds that watching a Tarzan matinee would be a fun thing to do, considering that fishing was now out of the question. After all, what kid growing up in America in the 1960s didn't want to grow up to be Tarzan?

After we cleaned up at our hotel and changed into some clean, dry clothes, we headed for the old Wabasha Theater. And, man, oh man, did we hit the jackpot. To our delight we discovered that it was a double feature: *Tarzan Goes to India* and *Tarzan's Three Challenges*, both of which starred Jock Mahoney as Tarzan. And what a Tarzan he was! From the moment the first movie started, I never again thought of anyone else as Tarzan. To me, Jock Mahoney *was* Tarzan, and he still is.

However, you may not be familiar with Jock Mahoney, so let me tell you a little bit about him. Jock Mahoney stood 6'4" and weighed 220 pounds of lithe, sculpted muscle, and he could move like a cat. Prior to being cast as Tarzan, he had been one of the leading stuntmen, if not *the* leading stuntman, in Hollywood for years and years, performing stunts for some of the most popular movie stars of the day—Errol Flynn, Randolph Scott, Tyrone Power, John Wayne, and many others. In fact, he had a reputation for doing stunts nobody else dared to do. He was sort of the Evel Kneivel of the stunt world.

For instance, Mahoney did a fight scene for western star Randolph Scott on top of a moving train. At one point Randolph Scott's character, whom Mahoney was doubling for, was supposed to knock the other guy off the train—*a real moving train, I might add.* As it turned out, the other stuntman was not willing to risk severe injury or quite possibly his life by taking the fall from the train. So they stopped filming, and Mahoney changed clothes with the other stuntman, then switched places, and ended the scene by being the guy knocked off the train. In the film, you see Mahoney knocking himself off the train. He told that story on Merv Griffin's television talk show in the late '70s after Griffin asked him what the most unusual stunt he had ever done was. The way Mahoney told the story was hilarious (more from Merv Griffin to come).

With that introduction to who Jock Mahoney was, it won't surprise you that in the beginning of the first feature, *Tarzan Goes to India*, you see Tarzan from behind in an open air biplane flying over the Bay of Bengal. When his pilot friend gives the signal, Tarzan taps him on the shoulder in gratitude and then jumps from the plane into the Bay of Bengal from about forty feet up. When he surfaces, he's waving good-bye with a big smile, and that was just the opening scene. From beginning to end, it was one incredible stunt after another with nonstop action as Tarzan saves a herd of elephants from certain annihilation with the help of a young boy named Jai. At one point Tarzan even wrestles a leopard with his bare hands. Bottom line: It is one incredible Tarzan movie.

When *Tarzan Goes to India* ended, Uncle Wally turned to my grandfather and said, "That guy was born to play Tarzan." And sure enough, my grandfather agreed.

After a short intermission, *Tarzan's Three Challenges* started. Whereas the first movie was filmed in India, this movie was filmed on location in Thailand and was an absolute visual masterpiece. But this movie had something even better going for it—the fact that it costarred none other than Woody Strode, one of Mahoney's real-life friends. Seriously, this film had the makings of being the greatest Tarzan film of all time. But something happened that made it all but impossible to complete.

On page 214 of Woody Strode's autobiography, *Goal Dust*, Strode explains exactly what happened during the filming of *Tarzan's Three Challenges*:

> *I spent five months in the jungles of Thailand working for Sy Weintraub. Jock Mahoney played Tarzan; he was the thirteenth Tarzan. He and I battle for control of the jungle.*
>
> *The final fight takes place on a rope net, like the square rigging of a ship laid flat, twelve feet off the ground. It took us five days to learn to balance and fight on that net.*
>
> *If you've ever seen that fight scene, you might notice that Jock Mahoney looks real skinny and sick, like the before picture in a Charles Atlas ad. Well, going into that picture, he* ***was*** *Charles Atlas, one of the strongest men in the world, a stuntman turned actor. But he jumped into the Klong River, the dirtiest river in the world, ten times worse than the worst open sewer, and caught tertiary malaria and amoebic dysentery.*
>
> *He was deathly sick; he couldn't eat. His lungs filled up with fluid and he developed pneumonia. After every fight scene we had to put him in an oxygen tent. Anybody else would have died but Jock Mahoney. I begged him not to go into that river, but he didn't believe he'd get sick; he believed he was Tarzan. That's what made him great.*
>
> *After the final scene, we rushed Jock from the jungle location in the back of a Land Rover. His body was burning up. A little Japanese girl working on the picture had a thermometer; his temperature was 104 degrees. When we got to the hotel, I picked*

him up and carried him inside. We put him in a tub and packed it with ice. I had some antibiotics and I fed those to him. It took the doctor an hour to show up. He asked me, "What have you done for him?"

I said, "I gave him some antibiotics."

He said, "Good!" and started to work on Tarzan. That's when we found out how sick he really was. Jock was lucky to survive.

Unfortunately, Jock Mahoney was so sick that he never played Tarzan again, but what a Tarzan he was. Check out those movies when you have a chance.

Here's why I've included Mahoney in the history section. Years later, Merv Griffin did a special television show on Tarzan in the movies, and he devoted more time to Jock Mahoney than anyone else. At one point he showed a clip of Mahoney wrestling a leopard in *Tarzan Goes to India*, and Griffin said, "My gosh, Jock, how many hours a day did you spend at the gym to look like that?" Mahoney just laughed and said, "I've never trained at a gym in my entire life, Merv. I just did what I always did since 1934, when I was a fifteen-year-old kid who wrote to Charles Atlas just like every other kid did." Griffin responded, "You mean, you looked like that from doing Isometrics?" Jock answered, "To the contrary, Isometrics was the least of it. Charles Atlas had you doing hundreds of push-ups, sit-ups, and deep knee bends every day. When I was training for Tarzan, I just did more, and I added a lot of swimming and rope climbing to it."

It was as simple as that, and yet it's what made Jock Mahoney a great Tarzan with a level of "off the charts" strength and fitness. And as you already know from reading about Charles Atlas, the push-up was Mahoney's foundation for lifetime strength and fitness.

Woody Strode

The first time I saw the great actor Woody Strode was on October 29, 1960, at the Orpheum Theater in downtown Minneapolis. I remember the date so clearly because it was a Saturday night, and we were celebrating my eighth birthday, which had actually fallen on Tuesday of that week. And celebrate we did. It could not have been a better or more memorable birthday, and part of the reason it was so memorable was because of the Kirk Douglas movie *Spartacus.*

It was a custom in our home that for our birthdays my mom and dad would take us to see the movie of our choice as long as it was either a biblical-type epic or a movie that starred John Wayne. On my brother Al's birthday six months earlier, we saw *Ben Hur: A Tale of the Christ*, and even now I can remember what it was like to watch the chariot race for the first time from the perspective of a seven-year-old. And now, six months later, it was my turn to choose.

Before I proceed, let me ask you a question. Have you seen the original 1960 movie version of *Spartacus*? If you haven't, you have missed the "#1 Manliest Movie" of all time according to *The Big Damn Book of Sheer Manliness*. And guess which scene more men remember than all others from that movie? If you've seen the film, you get three guesses, and two don't count. If you've not seen it, I'll wet your whistle for renting it. It's when the consummately evil Romans force Draba, the Ethiopian gladiator, to fight Spartacus to the death for their amusement and entertainment.

When I saw Draba, who was played perfectly by none other than the great Woody Strode, I was in awe. Even though I was only eight years old, I turned to my dad and said, "Daddy, he gots muscles just like Uncle Milo." Naturally, my uncle heard me and cracked up, but I could tell that he liked hearing it. And believe me, any man would, because Woody Strode had one of the all-time greatest physiques ever created as a collaboration between God and man.

In this particular scene, when the Romans pick Spartacus and Draba to fight each other to the death, I was literally on the edge of my seat as the scene began to unfold. Why? Because even as an eight-year-old, I didn't think that it was even remotely possible that Spartacus could beat Draba. So I was on the edge of my seat watching Spartacus and Draba fighting it out to the death in the arena, when suddenly I felt my dad's hand on my shoulder and heard him whisper into my ear, "Don't worry, little fella, there's more than two hours left. Spartacus isn't going to

die." Dad was right, of course. Even though Draba won, he refused to kill Spartacus and instead sacrificed his own life to save Spartacus by attacking the Romans until he himself was cut down. Truth be told, it was then and there that I became a huge fan of Woody Strode.

After *Spartacus*, the next time I remember seeing Woody was in John Ford's *Sergeant Rutledge* and then *The Man Who Shot Liberty Valance*, starring John Wayne. A year later I saw him in *Tarzan's Three Challenges*, which he starred in with his buddy Jock Mahoney, who played Tarzan (I told you all about it in the Jock Mahoney profile). Then I began to look for him and see him in more and more films and from time to time on television shows such as *Daniel Boone, Rawhide,* and *Tarzan*. In virtually every case, the famous Woody Strode physique was written into the script. And what a physique it was. It didn't matter whether he was in *Sargeant Rutledge*

or *The Professionals*, in which he finally broke through the racial barrier and received top billing ahead of Burt Lancaster, or in *The Last Rebel*, a spaghetti western in which he starred with NFL star quarterback Joe Namath, or his all-time greatest film, *Black Jesus*, for which he won critical acclaim. Bottom line: Woody Strode was one incredible actor, and he made a profound impact on everyone who saw him.

So now let's get to the point that relates to us and about how Woody Strode trained to develop his awesome physique. In his autobiography, *Goal Dust*, he first tells about his days as a star college athlete in both track and field and football for UCLA. It was during his time at UCLA that he created his own world-class strength and fitness program that was comprised of just three specific exercises.

This is what Strode states on page 42 of *Goal Dust*: "I picked up twenty pounds by doing one thousand push-ups a day. The school didn't allow us to lift weights. The coaches thought weightlifting would slow you down. So I developed natural strength from working out with my own body weight. I got so I could do a thousand push-ups, a thousand sit-ups, and a thousand knee squats every day. With the push-ups, I'd have to rest after every one hundred. The others I could do without stopping. I got into the knee squats because of a wrestler named Gama. He was an Indian wrestler who built this tremendous body by doing five thousand knee squats continuously. It would go on so long they would serve him tea."

So there you have it. That's exactly how Woody Strode created his incomparable physique. No weights, no gym, no equipment, and no foolin'. Just exactly what you see presented here in this book.

Dr. Miguelito Quixote Loveless

Robert Conrad

THE WILD, WILD WEST

From September 1965 to April 1969, my favorite television show was *The Wild, Wild West,* starring Robert Conrad. It was the one show that my friends and I tried to never miss. In fact, it was because of Robert Conrad, the star of *The Wild, Wild West,* that I began studying the martial arts in earnest in 1967.

Now for those of you who don't know anything about it, *The Wild, Wild West* was like watching a James Bond episode set in the American Old West. And just like a James Bond movie, it featured all kinds of cool gadgets, beautiful women, and some of the all-time best and most memorable villains in television history—some of whom showed up frequently. The most memorable was Dr. Miguelito Quixote Loveless, a brilliant but megalomaniac dwarf played perfectly by Michael Dunn. Dr. Loveless seemed to be modeled after Professor James Moriarty from Sherlock Holmes' fame, with the same type of maniacal "chip on his shoulder" desire to get rid of James West that Moriarty had for getting rid of Holmes. He made a fantastic, if not laugh your butt off funny, adversary for James West, similar to Wile E. Coyote in the Road Runner cartoons. And just like "The Coyote," it always seemed that try as he might, Dr. Loveless always managed to undo himself by the end of every episode. *Curses, foiled again.*

There were certain other *Wild, Wild West* standards that made it a favorite show among teenage boys. For instance, we knew for certain that James West (Robert Conrad) was a good guy through and through, and that he was going to be in at least two good fight scenes in every episode in which he did some serious butt kicking against thoroughly despicable characters usually played by guys like Bruce Dern, who deserved everything he gave them. In each fight scene Conrad would display his expertise in the martial arts. Conrad had all the moves, and there was absolutely no doubt that he could handle himself in real life. We also knew there would be several love scenes with some of the most beautiful women on television. There was never any doubt but that whenever a lovely lady showed up, James West (who incidentally always had a great tan) would have his shirt off, showing his absolutely perfect and flawless physique to best advantage. Bottom line: Conrad was an inspiration to young guys who wanted to grow up strong and fit, and he was the perfect advertisement for martial arts training.

So how do you suppose that Robert Conrad achieved such a perfect physique? Well, considering that you are reading this short biography in *Living Strength Ultimate Push-ups for the Awesome Physique*, it would probably have something to do with push-ups, don't you think?

Seriously, though, in the June 1994 edition of *Masters of Kung Fu* magazine, Conrad is featured on the cover and in an excellent article titled, "The Return of a TV Martial Arts Master." One of the questions they asked him about was how he trained for *The Wild, Wild West,* for which he did all of his own stunts. Conrad answered, *"What I would do primarily was train my body. I did road work. I did a lot of sit-ups and push-ups. I also did Isometric exercises. There was no pumping iron. I'm not saying you should or shouldn't. I just didn't do that."*

This verified what I had read about him in several other articles over the years. Robert Conrad always looked in incredible shape in every part he ever played. To this day I can't imagine anyone else playing the role of French trapper and explorer Pasquinel in James Michener's 1978 TV miniseries *Centennial.* And YES, he had his shirt off in a few scenes there too.

Simply put, the man was an example of what manly strength and fitness should be. And the push-up was his foundational exercise.

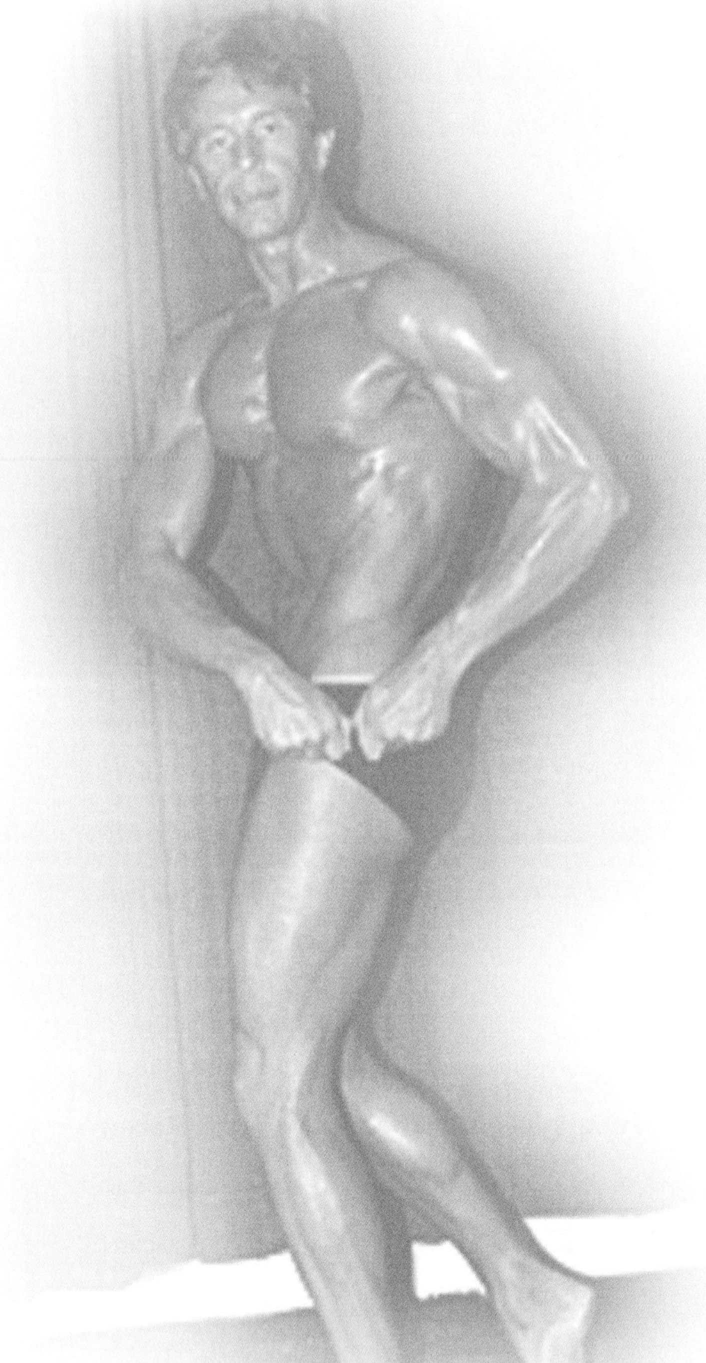

Jack King

IT'S TOO SOON TO QUIT

"I love those who can smile in trouble, who can gather strength from distress, and grow brave by reflection. 'Tis the business of little minds to shrink, but they whose heart is firm, and whose conscience approves their conduct, will pursue their principles unto death."

LEONARDO DA VINCI

I first read about Jack King in May 2001, when I received a phone call from a good friend of mine named Bryant. The first thing he said was, "Hey, John, it turns out that you and your grandpa and uncles were right all along." Naturally, hearing that I had been right was very gratifying, but I was curious to know what I had been right about. So I asked him and Bryant said, "Bill Starr has an article in the new issue of *Iron Man*, and he says the greatest physical transformations he had ever seen were with two guys who did nothing but push-ups. Can you believe that?" Naturally, without batting an eye, I said, "Are you kidding me, Bryant? I was telling you that more than 30 years ago when we were in high school, and back then you said the only reason that my uncles and I got the results we did from push-ups and Charles Atlas's exercises was because of our genetics. But do me a big favor and bring that article over when you can, because I'd like to read it for myself."

When Bryant arrived I couldn't help but get a kick out of his enthusiasm. And sure enough, Bill Starr had written a fantastic article that underscored the sensational benefits and results he had personally witnessed in seeing two men develop fantastic physiques as the result of going on a high volume push-up blitzing routine. What was most amazing was that although both men had achieved an incredible level of development, the one man, Jack King, was more than 35 years older than the other man when he began and had gone on to win the Masters Mr. America five years later in 1997, when he was 61 years old—due in no small part to his high volume push-up training that he used to sculpt his chest, arms, and shoulders.

This is exactly what Bill Starr had to say about Jack King: *"My longtime friend Jack King of Winston-Salem, North Carolina, is a perfect example. After recovering from a near-death experience, he found he couldn't do any free weight exercises for his upper body: no flat benches, inclines, declines—nothing. So how in the world was he going to maintain and improve his chest, shoulders, and arms? That was important to him because he'd switched his interest from Olympic weightlifting to competitive bodybuilding. Without arms, shoulders, and a chest, he wasn't going to have much of a chance.*

"He experimented, failed, experimented some more and, finally, came up with an exercise he could do without pain that brought him the desired results. It was a form of push-up, in which he placed his feet on a bench and did partial movements while he gripped blocks to take the pressure off his wrists. By adding reps, he slowly worked up to four sets of 150 reps. It worked wonderfully because he won a great many physique titles, including the Masters Mr. America."

I was so impressed by Bill Starr's article and, in particular, Jack King's story, that I referred to it in my book *Pushing Yourself to Power* that was published in 2003. Then, as I was in the process of writing this book, I decided to contact Mr. King personally and ask him a few specific questions about how he had trained, his near-death experience, and why it was that he ended up turning to the particular push-up variation that he had used in order to attain the astounding results that Mr. Starr had documented. As I talked with Jack, I discovered that his story was even more remarkable than I had anticipated. This is what he told me.

Jack King was born on February 3, 1936. As a boy, he always felt small for his age and never excelled at anything athletic. But that all changed when Jack was 14 years old, the year he became hooked on exercise. It all started one day when out of the blue he decided to run home from school, a distance of about a mile and a half. Although he had never done any serious running previously, he discovered that he really enjoyed the good feelings he felt from exercise and discussed it with a friend. When the school year ended, his friend informed him that he would be gone all summer and offered to let Jack use his 75-pound barbell during the summer months. Jack was very interested, but he didn't know the first thing about weightlifting. So Jack picked up two bodybuilding magazines at a local newsstand and began practicing exercises that he saw featured in the magazines. Before long he found himself capable of feats of strength that were far beyond any of his peers. And for the first time, Jack discovered he could excel at something physically—strength building.

Four years later, when Jack was 18, he saw an ad for instruction in Olympic weightlifting at the local YMCA. He decided to check it out, and in doing so he discovered a new passion to which he would dedicate himself, Olympic weightlifting. It was during his quest for Olympic style weightlifting excellence that in 1961 at the age of 25, Jack was first introduced to the steroid Dianabol. Dianabol had been created by Dr. John Zeigler and was originally created for use by the lifters of the York Barbell Club. Similar to many young lifters, Jack didn't know much about Dianabol or steroids in general. He was aware that they were being used by some of the best lifters in the world, especially those from York, Pennsylvania, and that they were totally safe, according to Dr. John Ziegler. In time, Jack also took another steroid called Winstrol. It was a combination of Dianabol and Winstrol that he took for many years.

When I specifically asked him about it, Jack said that he did not believe that the use of steroids alone actually made him stronger, because it had been documented through extensive scientific research that if one did not strength train when using steroids, there would be no noticible increase in muscular strength. But he did notice almost immediately that Dianabol speeded his recovery time in an incredible way and made it possible for him to train far more frequently and with far greater intensity. It was the dramatic effects as relates to recovery time that made extraordinary strength gains possible as the result of using steroids. In fact, Jack became so adept and powerful at his Olympic lifts that in time he found himself competing in the 198-pound class and setting record after record in meets. He became so strong that he got to the point that he could press more than 300 pounds, clean and jerk 340, and snatch 260. Bottom line: Pound for pound, Jack King had become one of the strongest men in the world.

But then one day in 1976, when Jack was 40 years old, he woke up feeling as though he was Superman in a room full of kryptonite. He was so weak he could hardly move and had to go to the hospital immediately. At first the doctors were perplexed and thought he had leukemia, then after further tests it was discovered that he was suffering from severe cases of hepatitis and mononucleosis simultaneously. He was even told by his doctor that no one had ever survived with their liver function so totally devastated and impaired. When his doctor asked him if he had been taking any type of drugs, Jack explained that he had been taking the two steroids. Naturally, Jack wondered if the steroids had caused his liver condition. His doctor replied, "No, Jack, the steroids didn't cause the hepatitis or mono, but they destroyed your immune system and made you susceptible to them."

Jack then told me, "My wife said the doctors had told her there was nothing they could do for me, so they told her to take me home because they thought I would be more comfortable if I died at home. They didn't give me any prescriptions, medications, nothing. I was totally on my own." It was then that something in his competitive nature kicked in, and Jack said to himself, "You're not gonna die. It's too soon to quit." He then became his own doctor and started taking Vitamin C as was recommended by famed researcher and two-time Nobel Prize laureate, Dr. Linus Pauling. Pauling recommended extremely high doses of Vitamin C when dealing with life-threatening illnesses, as much as 20,000 milligrams (20 grams) each day, which is exactly what Jack took. In addition, he also took 2,400 international units of natural Vitamin E daily, and slowly but surely Jack King beat all the odds and returned to full health and complete liver function. Once he had regained his health, Jack resumed his weightlifting. This time, he did so without the use of steroids.

Fast forward to 1991. Although Jack had survived his close encounter with death and was able to return to the weightlifting exercise that he so deeply enjoyed, over the next 15 years, he began to be plagued by a series of painful injuries to his joints. So much so, that by the end of 1991, he found himself experiencing excruciating pain and injury to his shoulders and wrists. It was this condition that Bill Starr had written about in his article in the June 2001 *Iron Man* magazine, where he stated, *"My longtime friend Jack King . . . found he couldn't do any free weight exercises for his upper body: no flat benches, inclines, declines—nothing. . . . finally, he came up with an exercise he could do without pain that brought him the desired results. It was a form of push-up, in which he placed his feet on a bench and did partial movements while he gripped blocks to take the pressure off his wrists. By adding reps, he slowly worked up to four sets of 150 reps. It worked wonderfully because he won a great many physique titles, including the Masters Mr. America."*

It was in early 1992 at the age of 56 that Jack took up high volume push-ups in earnest and discovered the power of push-ups not only to transform his physique but to also heal his shoulders and the joints of his upper body. In fact, on his high volume push-up days, which were Wednesdays and Saturdays, Jack would often perform 1,500 or more repetitions, and he told me that on one particular Saturday he performed 2,000 repetitions for no other reason than just to prove to himself that he could do that many. Out of curiosity, I asked him, "Jack, at what point did you decide to elevate your feet when doing your push-ups?" His response was, "John, at the very beginning when I tried doing them with my feet on the floor, the angle was totally wrong and caused me too much pain in my shoulders. But then I discovered that with my feet elevated to about 19" on an exercise bench that the angle was just right, and I could get a perfect pump in my arms, chest, shoulders, and upper back without much pain at all. And then after a few months went by, I realized that I had no pain at all. Absolutely none." I then asked him, "Jack, how did your physique compare once you mastered high volume push-ups to what it had been from weight training?" His immediate response was "Better!"

In fact, it wasn't long after making push-ups the cornerstone and foundation of his upper body bodybuilding program that Jack began competing in major bodybuilding contests and winning. Three times he was awarded first place in the tall man's division (Jack's 5'10-1/2") of the Masters Mr. America Contest. The icing on the cake came in 1997 when at the age of 61, Jack was awarded first place and declared the overall winner of the Masters Mr. America contest.

Since that time, Jack has continued to train, and at the age of 77 he can still outperform men who are less than a third his age. To this day Jack will tell you that in terms of creating a beautifully sculpted upper body, you can't do better than high volume push-ups. And if anyone should know, it's Jack King.

"I have been impressed with the urgency of doing.
Knowing is not enough; we must apply.
Being willing is not enough; we must do."

LEONARDO DA VINCI

chapter THREE

guide

Your Personal Guide to Push-up Self-Mastery

"To be nobody but yourself in a world which is doing its best, night and day, to make you just like everybody else means to fight the hardest battle which any human being can fight; and never stop fighting."

E. E. CUMMINGS

Your Personal Guide to Push-up Self-Mastery

Having read the success profiles in the previous chapter, I'm sure that most of you are convinced that the push-up really is "The King" of all upper body exercises. And I'm also sure that many of you are motivated to the extreme and would really like to "jumpstart" your own "miracle transformation" just as soon as possible, if not sooner. But before you do, we want you to test yourself in order to see whether or not you can perform at least 50 (but preferably 75 to 100) consecutive push-ups in good form without pushing yourself to the absolute limit of exhaustion and having to spend the rest of the day in an oxygen tent. If you can't, I want you to spend at least the next 28 days on this personalized custom

program that I am about to present to you *before* you go about mastering any of the other courses in *Living Strength Training System*. Why 28 days? Because in all but the most extreme cases, you'll be knocking off sets of 50 plus push-ups in perfect form by the end of week four. And in all likelihood you will be able to perform 75 to 100 by the end of week seven if you apply yourself to our program for that length of time. Believe me, I know what I'm talking about.

As you will soon discover, there is a good reason for this. That reason is because the push-up is the foundational exercise upon which the entire *Living Strength Training System* is built. No other exercise in the entire realm of Physical Culture works the upper body musculature as synergistically including chest, shoulders, arms, upper/lower back, and abs as well as the push-up (especially our own signature Living Strength Push-up). And though it is absolutely true that every program in our entire *Living Strength Training System* will yield fantastic results, those results will be amplified many times over by making the push-up the foundational exercise upon which everything else is built. This was true for all of the great bodybuilding courses of the early twentieth century, including the original Charles Atlas Course, Earle Liederman's Course, Edwin Checkley's Course, and Bernarr MacFadden's Course, among others, and it is just as true of *Living Strength*. Also bear in mind that the push-up was the foundational exercise of all the men featured in chapter 2, such as Jack King, Woody Strode, Jock Mahoney, Robert Conrad, Charles Atlas, and every other man featured in this book. It will also be true of YOU. So much so that if you decided to do nothing but just this one specific program that we are about to outline for the rest of your life, you would still achieve fantastic results. With that in mind, our goal from here on out with this course is to build your foundation for lifelong strength and fitness. In fact, I'll make this promise to you. If, for whatever reason, you decide to do nothing but this program for the rest of your life, you will still achieve fantastic, even world-class results, and everyone will do a double take when they see you and ask how you achieved such a fine physique and obvious strength and fitness. At that point you might tell them something like, "I do 500 Living Strength Push-ups every day," while they stand there dumbfounded and look at you in sheer disbelief. And believe me, I'm not overstating it. To most people

500 push-ups is in the realm of dreams and the idea of doing 1,000 is incomprehensible, but *it won't be for you anymore, because you will be the living proof.*

Now as you have already learned in reading the success profiles related to Greg Newton in the introduction, Charles Atlas, Woody Strode, Robert Conrad, Jock Mahoney, and Jack King, no single exercise in the entire realm of body weight Physical Culture exercise takes the place of the push-up. *One hundred (100) consecutive repetitions in good form was the gold standard that all these men aspired to achieve. It separated the men from the boys. It still does.* The question is, how do you rate?

The right answer in 28 to 49 days will be *"Absolutely great!"* if you follow our push-up program to the letter as outlined. In fact, it's all but "foolproof."

All right, so let's get to it. Our first order of business within the next 28 to 49 days is to get you to at least 50 but preferably 75 to 100 consecutive reps in good form. Right now, you may actually be thinking that you're not planning on challenging your Army Ranger buddy like my friend Dwight Hall to a push-up contest. All you really want is to transform your physique in world-record time. Am I right? So why should you bother hitting the deck and giving me 75 to 100 push-ups before moving on? I'll tell you why. Because if you train exactly as we outline here, this push-up program will "volumize" your upper body muscles with highly oxygenated blood that is full of vital growth factors and nutrients that will help to fill out your pectorals, deltoids, triceps, and even tighten your abs faster than an Army Ranger recruit can clean a latrine with a toothbrush. In addition, it will stimulate and maximize manly male hormone (testosterone) production and the release of HGH, both of which give you that elusive fountain of youth. Not only that, but when you can knock off sets of 75 to 100 reps of the standard military variety, you will then be able to notch it up dramatically and perform sets of 35 to 50 super advanced Living Strength Push-ups in succession, and at that point you'll be able to take on any program you want to take on.

But first you need a foundation, and this is it. Not only that, but in the process of sculpting your physique with this specific program, you will also have dramatically enhanced your lung capacity and achieved an incredible level of cardiovascular development while also enhancing full body muscular definition. This added level of superior strength and stamina will also carry over into your athletic pursuits. After all, how could it not?

The Science That Validates the Truth

Back in the early 1960s there was an exercise physiologist by the name of Dr. Laurence E. Morehouse who was the professor of kinesiology and founding director of the Human Performance Laboratory at the University of California at Los Angeles (UCLA). At the time Dr. Morehouse was working with America's astronauts in the Apollo Space Program to determine the best conditioning program for them to use in order to enhance prolonged work capacity while they were in space.

At first he and his associates were testing ultraintense, short-duration strength training in the form of Isometric Contraction, which had been validated as the ultimate strength training method by Drs. E. A. Mueller and Theodore Hettinger of the Max Planck Institute in Dortmund, Germany, during the 1950s and early '60s. The primary reason Isometric Contraction was chosen and tested was because it had a distinct advantage over every other training modality in that it could be effectively performed without reliance on gravity or bulky equipment while in a zero gravity space environment. Unfortunately, Dr. Morehouse and his team soon discovered that while Isometric Contraction builds the contractile proteins within the muscle fiber to facilitate immediate and incredible strength gains, it does not dramatically enhance the endurance capacity of the working muscle for prolonged muscular work when the contractions are maintained for a duration lasting only six to twelve seconds. For that reason it was then decided that Isometric Contraction could be best utilized while the astronauts were in space by using a small Isometric Training device called an Exer-Genie that Dr. Morehouse invented in order to maintain strength and prevent muscular atrophy, but that it was not the best way to enhance overall work capacity in preparation for the space flight. In fact, it was then that Dr. Morehouse and his collegues tested and subsequently discovered that high volume, moderate intensity, multi-joint strength training, such as is performed when doing a Standard Military Push-up, releases the brakes and kicks into gear the other wheels of muscle metabolism. Or to put it more succinctly, moderate intensity, high volume, multi-joint strength work, of which the Standard Military style Push-up is a perfect example, is the quickest way to achieve an astonishing level of accelerated muscle growth and strength/endurance work capacity.

Why is this the case? Because the volume of sarcoplasm (the muscle cell's jello-like filler) goes way up while the mitochondria, the muscle cell's energy power plants, move into super high gear and become highly efficient. Simultaneous to this, there is an intense capillarization that also takes place as the capillaries spread their tentacles throughout the muscle. In other words, the blood supply feeding the muscles is dramatically increased, thus bringing highly oxygenated, nutrient rich blood, complete with growth and healing factors to the working muscles. This makes it possible for the muscles to work both harder and longer without fatigue, causing not only an increase in muscle size but also a dramatic increase in both strength and endurance capacity simultaneously. This is what I refer to as *functional strength.* It is literally the ability to sustain high-level muscular activity for extended periods of time without becoming unduly fatigued or exhausted. This is exactly what Dr. Morehouse was looking for as relates to America's astronauts. They needed to be able to work long hours without undo fatigue.

Now when you stop to think about Dr. Morehouse's research in the light of what was stated in the previous chapter outlining the success profiles of Charles Atlas, Jack King, Woody Strode, Jock Mahoney, and Robert Conrad, who themselves had experienced firsthand exactly what Dr. Morehouse's research validated, it all lines up and makes perfect sense. This then brings us to one last but very inspiring story that we'd like to share with you before we give you your very own personalized custom program that will take you all the way to push-up excellence. The reason we are sharing it with you here instead of in the previous chapter is because we did not know the name of

the young man who was featured in the same story that Bill Starr wrote in *Iron Man* about Jack King. Therefore, we could not write a success profile naming him by name. And besides, I wanted to inspire you to the maximum just before you start your own program and show you that even if you can't do more than a few push-ups at the beginning, it won't matter in the least. *All that really does matter is that you have the guts, determination, and persistence to see this program through for at least 28 days.* If you do that, we're certain that you won't want to stop because you will be thrilled with your results. And success begets success. So here goes.

The Genesis of This Program

As I already related to you in Jack King's success profile, it all started back in May 2001, when I received a phone call from a good friend of mine named Bryant. The first thing he said was, "Hey, John, it turns out that you and your grandpa and uncles were right all along." Naturally, hearing that I had been right was very gratifying, but I was curious to know what I had been right about. So I asked him, and you know the rest. Bryant said, "Bill Starr has an article in the new issue of *Iron Man*, and he says the greatest physical transformations he had ever seen were with two guys who did nothing but push-ups. Can you believe that?" Naturally, without batting an eye, I said, "Are you kidding me, Bryant? I was telling you that more than 30 years ago when we were in high school, and back then you said the only reason that my uncles and I got the results we did from push-ups and Charles Atlas's self-resistance exercises was because of our genetics. But do me a big favor and bring that article over when you can, because I'd like to read it for myself."

When Bryant arrived with the article, I was amazed, to say the least. Here in a bodybuilding magazine that was filled from cover to cover with photos of some of the most grossly overdeveloped and chemically enhanced physiques I had ever seen was an article by strength coach extraordinaire, the legendary Bill Starr. And in the article he told the stories of two real-life men whom he personally knew who had both achieved extraordinary results from an intensive high volume push-up specialization routine. The first one you already know about, my friend—Masters Mr. America, Jack King—and the second one was a young man Starr met when he was stationed in Iceland while he was serving in the United States Air Force. This is what he said:

"I saw a great example of progressive resistance at work when I was in the Air Force stationed in Iceland. A corporal had allowed himself to fall into a terrible physical state. Upon arriving at the island he'd stopped all forms of exercise and started indulging himself to the maximum. Within six months he'd gained 50 pounds, all of it ugly weight. When he became eligible for a furlough back to the States, he altered his lifestyle. It seemed he'd only been married a week before shipping off to Iceland, and he wanted to look his best when he went home. He stopped drinking alcohol, cut back on his eating, and started doing one exercise—push-ups. His reason for choosing them was different from Jack's [referring to Jack King]. We didn't have a bench in our tiny gym, and he recalled how effective push-ups had been for him in basic training. He was in such sad shape that all he could manage the first time was 15 reps, but he had a couple things going for him. He was extremely motivated, and he was young. Slowly but consistently he added more reps to each set, then started doing multiple sets. Every time I saw him on base—in the rec room, the mess hall, the barracks—he'd drop down and do a set. He got to where he could do 75 in a set, and over the course of a day he'd sometimes do more than 1,500.

"He was using progressive resistance training just by increasing his reps, and he altered his physique in a remarkable way. I've never seen anyone transform his body so radically, so rapidly. After less than a month on his push-up blitz, he had muscular arms, chest, and shoulders. In the process of doing so many reps, he also tightened his midsection, and his upper back stood out in bold relief. He looked as though he'd been doing some serious advanced level bodybuilding for some time."

Now, let me state something that I have often stated before. I have great respect for

Bill Starr and his many accomplishments, but I'm amazed every time I read his last sentence. *"He looked as though he'd been doing some serious advanced level bodybuilding for some time."*

Why am I saying that? Because to me it's obvious that the young man in question *was* doing some very serious advanced level bodybuilding? I mean, c'mon, the guy was knocking off up to 1,500 push-ups in a day just like Jack King had done, and he had achieved the most radical and rapid muscular transformation that Bill Starr had ever witnessed. If that's not extremely fast and advanced bodybuilding with the results to prove it, then would someone be kind enough to enlighten me and let me know what is?

Now, with that inspiration to motivate you, let's create a customized push-up program that is uniquely customized to YOU and you alone.

Your Personalized Program to Push-up Mastery

What follows is the Push-up Interval Training Program that I first learned from Dr. Laurence E. Morehouse back in 1977, which he briefly mentioned in his best-seller, *Maximum Performance*, though he did not give specific details. As a young martial arts instructor, I wanted to get my students in fighting shape as quickly as possible using his program. So I literally called him at UCLA and kept on calling him until I finally reached him and got the exact details of how best to structure the program for students of my own.

First, let me say that Dr. Morehouse was a great guy with a marvelous sense of humor, and it was fortunate for me that he liked the fact that I was so tenacious. When I first talked with him about the push-up program that he had briefly mentioned in *Maximum Performance*, he was very pleased that I had picked up on it and that I wanted the details. He said that he had originally developed the program for America's early astronauts, then he fondly reminisced about working with our astronauts and told me that they were the most unique breed of men he had ever met. He said that although they were highly individualistic, they were also totally dedicated to one another's welfare unlike any group of people he had met before or since. Nearly all of them had been fighter pilots in either WWII or the Korean War and then had become test pilots. Most were practical jokers and were always playing pranks on one another.

Morehouse stated that they were the highest testosterone, most driven and competitive group of men that he had ever met—always trying to outdo one another and constantly pushing to the edge of the edge of what had been done or could be done. As such, he said it was great fun to be around them, to experience their energy, and to work with them, but the first thing he realized was, as he put it, "No way was anyone going to tell these guys to go to a gym and to train under someone else's supervision. Not when you've got a guy such as Alan Shepherd looking you in the eye and telling you, 'Look, Doc, I'm gonna be flying it and not lifting it, so just tell me how to get in the best shape for flying it, and I'll do it.'" In a sense, that made Dr. Morehouse's job a great deal easier, because in spite of the fact that these men were representing the most technologically advanced nation the world had ever produced, they were totally down to earth and grounded.

Dr. Morehouse added, "To a man they each believed in God, family, and the American way. There was no way they were going to let the Soviets beat us into space if they could help it. As such, they lived a no-frills existence and wanted everything broken down to its most essential and practical terms. They weren't interested in theories, and they never did anything in ten steps when they could do it in one. As relates to physical conditioning, these men were already motivated, because they each wanted to be the first man on the moon." All Dr. Morehouse really had to do was clearly state the objective and explain to these men why they needed to develop a great reserve of muscular strength and endurance in order to compensate for the lost strength and muscle that they would definitely experience as the result of spending prolonged time in a weightless space environment. The fact is that once they understood the logic behind what they were being asked to do, they all followed through on their own far beyond anyone's expectation and achieved astounding results.

After hearing Dr. Morehouse's story about the astronauts, I couldn't wait to get the specific details. Once I had them in hand, I personally applied his program with extraordinary results as did several of my martial arts friends and students. And as you will soon see, Dr. Morehouse's program also has a great deal in common with the program that Bill Starr mentioned had been used by the young corporal in Iceland. The only real difference is that Dr. Morehouse's program is a very comprehensive and structured program that is uniquely individualized for you and you alone. This more than anything else makes it the best and most comprehensive push-up program in existence. This brings up a good point: don't compare yourself to anyone else. It does not even remotely matter how many push-ups your friends can or cannot do. All that matters is that you reach your own best standard as quickly as possible, which you will do with this program. So let's jump in.

1 MONDAY

Monday Is Test Day

Your program starts out on Monday morning of each week. The first thing you'll do after practicing your Living Strength deep breathing exercises is to perform a single test set of the Military Push-up. So hit the deck. Using as close to flawless form as possible (see the photos), with the standard feet on the floor Military Push-up, you will perform one set to your absolute limit of good form. When you start to lose form, quit! Write that number down.

NOTE: Though we have based this foundational program on using the Standard Military Push-up (variation #4) as our foundational exercise, there may be a number of men who are not *yet* strong enough to perform Military Push-ups in their daily workouts. If you happen to be one of them, don't despair. Instead of starting out with the Military Push-up, you will use one of our less intense variations, such as the Ron Watson (an injured Vietnam veteran whom I highly admire) variation #1 found at the end of this chapter (just before the charts). Among the variations you will discover there are seven in all that can be used interchangeably, depending upon current strength and fitness levels. You'll also notice that the Military Push-up is variation #4. In other words, it is for men who are already reasonably strong and fit and who wish to become super strong and fit. Also note there are three less intense variations and three more intense variations with the Military Push-up placed in the middle. If you are rehabbing from an injury or are just starting out, we recommend you start at level #1 or #2 and stay with each level until you can perform at least 50 reps (but preferably 75>) in good form before moving to the next level and continue until you can perform the Standard Military Push-up for at least 15 repetitions in perfect form. At that point you can then use the program exactly as specified in the charts until you do 50 to 75 with no problem. If you can already do 75 or more Military Push-ups, then use one of the advanced feet elevated variations. And if you can perform 100 consecutive Living Strength Push-ups in good form, please send us your pictures and contact information so that we can have you model in future books and courses.

Now look at the following charts for Weeks 1–4.

WEEK 1

DAY	INTERVAL INTENSITY	REST INTERVAL
MONDAY (TEST 100% MAX)	35%	60 MINUTES
TUESDAY	50%	60 MINUTES
WEDNESDAY	60%	60 MINUTES
THURSDAY	30%	60 MINUTES
FRIDAY	50%	60 MINUTES
SATURDAY	40%	60 MINUTES
SUNDAY	25%	90 MINUTES

WEEK 2

DAY	INTERVAL INTENSITY	REST INTERVAL
MONDAY (TEST 100% MAX)	40%	60 MINUTES
TUESDAY	65%	90 MINUTES
WEDNESDAY	50%	60 MINUTES
THURSDAY	70%	120 MINUTES
FRIDAY	40%	60 MINUTES
SATURDAY	50%	60 MINUTES
SUNDAY	30%	120 MINUTES

WEEK 3

DAY	INTERVAL INTENSITY	REST INTERVAL
MONDAY (TEST 100% MAX)	40%	60 MINUTES
TUESDAY	50%	60 MINUTES
WEDNESDAY	75%	90 MINUTES
THURSDAY	45%	60 MINUTES
FRIDAY	80%	120 MINUTES
SATURDAY	60%	90 MINUTES
SUNDAY	25%	90 MINUTES

WEEK 4

DAY	INTERVAL INTENSITY	REST INTERVAL
MONDAY (TEST 100% MAX)	90%	120 MINUTES
TUESDAY	45%	60 MINUTES
WEDNESDAY	35%	60 MINUTES
THURSDAY	65%	90 MINUTES
FRIDAY	80%	120 MINUTES
SATURDAY	35%	90 MINUTES
SUNDAY	20%	120 MINUTES

Note the percentage of maximum that you will be performing each day and the time intervals of rest between each set. For instance, on Monday of week one, after you perform one maximum test set, you will be performing sets at 35% of your max at one-hour intervals throughout the day. (We have all the percentages and numbers they equate to charted out for you on the last two pages of this course so you don't have to guess.) For example, let's say that you're in really good shape and performed 50 reps in flawless form. 50 reps X 35% = 17.5 reps. So, every hour between your early morning test set and an hour before bedtime, you'll knock off one set of 17 or 18 reps. In the course of a day, that's somewhere between 170 and 216 reps.

On Tuesday, you start knocking off sets at 50% of your Monday test maximum. So that means 25 reps every hour. This, in turn, means that by the end of the day you will have knocked off somewhere between 250 to 300 reps. But note: You never once approached your maximum. This is key because you want to build and maximize strength/endurance while volumizing your muscles with highly oxygenated blood and yet do so without overtaxing your central nervous system. In fact, if you overtax your CNS, you will be setting yourself back and not advancing as quickly as you would if you followed the program to the letter.

"Everything should be made as simple as possible, but not simpler."

Albert Einstein

You will then continue each day exactly as specified on the charts, mixing up both the speed and intensity of each set and the duration of rest periods between sets. Any time you have a question about how many reps a given percentage equates to, just go to pages 80-81 of this course and look it up. Test yourself only on Mondays and do the easy sets as prescribed for the rest of that day. You are going to get hooked on the constant pump. We know, because we are and have been hooked for more years than many of you guys reading this have been alive.

Do the best you can to maintain the schedule outlined in the charts, but don't have a "hissy fit" if you miss your appointment with the concrete or carpet from time to time. Make it up if you can, but don't sweat it if you can't. Do your sets from the time you get up in the morning until one hour before bedtime. Naturally, while you're at work or in school you will have a couple of gaps in your day when you can't drop and pump out a set of push-ups. Don't worry about it. Just get back on schedule whenever you can.

NOTE: *It is extremely important that you go to your limit only once each week on your test day. Performing sets to "absolute failure" on a routine basis is a recipe for failure for any beginner. Why? Because doing so overstresses your central nervous system and puts your joints and connective tissues in harm's way. Why is that the case? Because in pushing your muscles to the point of absolute failure, they lose their protective function and then your joints, ligaments, and tendons have nothing to protect them. Dumb. Dumb. Dumb! So don't do it and don't mess with the outline; stay well within your ability except on test days! And then you will perform only one maximum set. Don't worry. You're going to make fantastic gains without collapsing on the last rep, dripping with sweat, and making noises and faces like a Neanderthal. This will become evident to you as your reps increase dramatically on your test days.*

The prescribed regimen requires that you say no to any other upper bodywork other than ab work until you master the Military Push-up for the

Jack Dempsey, *World Heavyweight Boxing Champion, 1919—1926*

first 4 to 7 weeks. At that point, if you can perform 75 reps in good form, you can then move up to other more intense variations or to the other Living Strength Training Courses for perfecting any body part that you desire. And if you are super ambitious, you can start performing the *Super Advanced Living Strength Push-up* as your foundational exercise. But don't think you need to or that you should, unless you want to, because it isn't absolutely necessary. And besides, you're welcome to stay with this program as long as you wish.

Now, let me make a further point. If your sport is mixed martial arts (MMA) or boxing, the push-up should be an indispensable part and foundation of your training arsenal. It was a key exercise in the training regimen of Jack Dempsey and Rocky Marciano (Dempsey and Marciano routinely knocked off sets of 50 reps), two of the hardest hitters in boxing history. And it is and has been the key exercise of Herschel Walker, former Heisman Trophy winner, NFL star running back of the 1980s and '90s, and who now at age 50 is a professional MMA fighter routinely competing against men half his age. And why is this so? Because relaxed shoulders are critical to the fluid transmission of power from the hip to the fist. Anyone who has ever put on a pair of boxing gloves and climbed into the square circle knows that holding your guard and punching for ten to twelve three-minute rounds will greatly exhaust the deltoid muscles of the shoulders and the biceps and triceps of the

Herschel Walker

Rocky Marciano

Antonino Rocca

arms. A fatigued muscle becomes a tight muscle. At the point of muscular fatigue, punches deteriorate into pushes as the deltoid muscles of the shoulder become too tired to hold up the arms, which in turn is exactly why the last rounds of some professional boxing bouts these days end up looking like an amateur brawl, where the two combatants are hanging all over each other. That never happened during Rocky Marciano's era from the early to mid 1950s. The "Rock" could go fifteen rounds with no clinches, and the punches never stopped. Which is also why today's boxers ought to go back to the tried and true push-up.

At the same time that Rocky Marciano was the World's Heavyweight Boxing Champion, Antonino Rocca was the International Heavyweight Wrestling Champion. In his 1957 course of bodybuilding and wrestling, Rocca stated that he performed 3 to 5 sets of 100 push-ups each day. He also stated that any man who could perform 100 Rocca's consecutively in good form would be among the top 2% of the strongest, best-conditioned athletes in the world.

Proper Push-Up Technique

Okay, let's talk push-up form. Whether you're training for the boxing ring, the beach, or the bodybuilding stage, proper push-up technique will amplify your gains.

In all, we have seven variations, ranging from the Less-Than-Intense Ron Watson variation #1 Push-up to the Super Intense Living Strength Push-up. For this program we are concentrating on the Standard Military Push-up with feet on the floor or the Super Advanced Living Strength variation. With either variation, place your weight near the bases of your palms rather than near the ends of your fingers. If the traditional technique hurts your wrists, you can use a set of push-up handles that are readily available at almost any sporting goods store. Or you can do your push-ups the martial arts way, on tight fists with your body weight resting on your knuckles. Now granted, if you're not planning on kicking some serious butt in the near future, you may wish to do your push-ups on the full surfaces of your fists. Or you may do them the way I was taught when we were moving through the martial arts ranks by resting your weight on the first two knuckles of each fist, those of the index and middle fingers. You'll find that this tough-as-nails technique will strengthen your wrists in

NOTE: This illustrates how your buttocks can get raised too high and not in a straight line from your shoulders to your heels.

a hurry, and noodle-thin wrists that scream for mercy in any sport endeavor, whether swinging a racquet, a golf club, or a baseball bat, will be a thing of the past.

This brings up another point. There are macho guys who like to prove how tough they are by doing everything to the extreme and putting themselves in harm's way. You know the type I mean. The kind of guy who sits at a bar someplace with his big gut hanging over his belt and bragging about how much he used to be able to bench press until he got too busted up to train any longer. Trust us on this—doing knuckle push-ups or plyometric knuckle push-ups on bare concrete will not amplify your gains one iota. Doing so will not prove that you are tough any more than eating broken glass and sleeping on a bed of nails will prove that you are tough. All that it will prove is that you are a very sick masochist or suicidally stupid. Take your pick. So don't do it.

When it comes to Standard Military Push-ups or the advanced variations that you'll be doing later, the grip width is up to you. But we recommend that you vary it from time to time or even from set to set. This will enhance results by stimulating further muscular adaptation from set to set.

Keep your butt tucked under, with your buttocks/glutes contracted tightly, your thighs together contracted hard, and your abdominals tight. This will make your push-ups look crisp and keep your body in a straight line from your shoulders to your heels, while it protects your lower back from sagging and hurting.

Do not constrict your chest (especially when doing the Living Strength Push-up variation) by looking straight down (look at

the photos and notice that I am looking straight ahead instead of down). Keep your chest wide open so that you can perform costal breathing and breathe as deeply as possible. Yes, we agree, the range of motion may be slightly enhanced, while at the same time your pectoral muscles will be prestretched for more power. I learned this as a kid from my uncles as relates to Atlas style (variation #5) Push-ups. They always said, "Johnny, look straight ahead and not down." Jack King, on the other hand started looking straight ahead when he began his high volume push-up blitzes, because he would touch his chest to the floor on each rep instead of taking it on the chin or nose. The other point, and this is significant, is that you are less likely to injure your shoulders that way. So remember to look straight ahead rather than straight down. Why does this seemingly insignificant adjustment amplify results so dramatically? Simple. Because maintaining tension in the neck extensor muscles will facilitate a much stronger contraction of the elbow extensors.

Next, learn to synchronize your breathing with your movement. Failing to do so will severely limit your output, and it's the kiss of death in any endurance event, especially high volume sets of push-ups and pull-ups. Under the circumstances, breathe as naturally as possible, but breathe deep. Really feel your chest expand with every breath. This was something I learned when I was a kid, and it made a big difference. My uncle Milo told me that once he got up to his high rep numbers of more than 100 reps per set that he wasn't even thinking about his breathing other than the fact that he was breathing deep. I have found the same thing to be true with my own breathing. When I perform high volume sets of the Living Strength variation

(see photo), I'm breathing naturally and not really thinking about it. Still, we do have one technique that may help you at first. It's a technique that comes from Edwin Checkley's "A Natural Method of Physical Training." In this technique, you inhale deeply into your chest as much as possible on the way down (the resting phase) and exhale with power on the way up (the exertion phase). Imagine your breath flowing out of your chest and into your arms and shoulders during the push. Believe me, there is plenty of evidence that scientifically validates the power of such visualization techniques when applied to any endeavor.

Once your numbers start to go up in a dramatic way, intentionally try to rest your muscles on the way down by lessening the tension during the down phase. For example, a first-rate endurance athlete such as an ultra marathon runner knows how to let his or her limbs recover between strides. Find your own rhythm ASAP and stick with it. You'll discover that once you are in *your zone* that a rhythmical, synchronized activity takes a lot less energy than a nonrhythmical one, thanks to something that God put in place in wiring the central nervous system of a human being that is scientifically referred to as "central pattern generators."

Another tip is to take advantage of the recoil effect at the bottom of the movement. Now don't get us wrong. We're not talking about "bouncing" off the bottom, far from it. We're talking about immediately contracting your muscles and moving from the bottom of the movement back to the top just short of locking out without breaking stride. This is not a bench press meet. There isn't anybody around to "red light" you at the bottom for failing to pause. So go to it and maintain your own natural rhythm.

When you finally get to the point where your weekly gains are not quite as dramatic as they were during the first few weeks as will be *evidenced on your test days,* it's time to regroup and bring out the accelerated *Isometric Tension Techniques*. These are to be used only on your test days and at no other time.

Accelerated Isometric Power Techniques

First, feel as though your hands are locked into the floor. This one takes a little bit of explaining and understanding. Have you ever watched a karateka generate extra power into his punches? He starts with his fist tightly clenched at his side, palm up, and close to his waistline. As he extends his fist forward and upward, he generates power by rotating his fist while the punch is being thrown. Upon full extension, his palm is then facing down. This added torque dramatically intensifies the power of the punch at impact. You will apply the same concept, but you will be applying the torque *Isometrically* from the inside out. Now to do this, I want you to first visualize breaking a stick over your knee. Note how your shoulders get externally rotated and adducted. *That is the exact action that you want to feel Isometrically.* As you grab the floor tight, apply torque to it. Generate it clockwise with your right hand and counter-clockwise with your left hand. Properly done, your hands will stay in position and don't move at all. But you will notice a wave of *dynamic tension* moving from your hands, through your forearms, to your upper arms, into your shoulders, and all the way to your lats and pecs. You will literally sense a burst of power by utilizing this technique when you need it most.

Second, clench your glutes hard and tighten your abs as hard as possible.

Third, squeeze your thighs tight together, contracting the thigh muscles as strongly as you can Isometrically.

Fourth, when you are at single final reps, I want you to hold your breath on exertion (the push) and exhale with power at the top. *You don't want to hold your breath while making a maximum effort for more than a few seconds, but we are only talking about a few seconds tops. So don't sweat it.*

Incorporate all four of these Isometric power techniques during the actual final reps to generate more power and push out of the last few reps. When utilizing these techniques, use your head and take a few breaths before the next rep if you need to while you are in the up position. Incorporating the above four techniques can easily add an additional three reps to your one set max the first time you try them. I repeat, these *Isometric power techniques* are to be utilized only during your maximum test sets. You're on your honor.

Now that you have come this far, you may decide to take on your Army Ranger buddy in a push-up contest after all. If you do, just stick with this program until you whip him. Once your body has fully adapted to daily push-ups, you may opt for some of the advanced and super advanced routines that follow. Or you may decide to utilize the exact same method in mastering other types of push-ups. The choice is yours. Just remember the rules of the push-up program.

The Rules of Push-Up Self-Mastery

Never come close to failure except on your test day when going for your one set maximum.

Vary the rep ranges and the rest periods between the sets daily.

Adjust the load to your recovery ability (if you need more time between sets than is listed in the charts, take it).

Build up cumulative fatigue. Taper down before a test day.

Conclusion

There you have it, my friend. Your complete, no excuses guide to push-up self-mastery and creating an "off the charts" strength-to-body-weight ratio. Put it to work and fill out your shirt before the month is up! Quite often our students have added 2" to 3" to their chests in just the first 28 days by practicing push-ups every day and following the Living Strength Super Nutrition Plan as specified. I realize that this advice may not sound all that trendy in our age of high tech machines and "total muscle failure" advocates, or especially considering those who advocate training just once in a blue moon. But our methods will transform you in world-record time just as it has for yours truly, and all the other men whom you read about throughout this book.

So hit the deck… and give us a hundred!

Anytime Warm-up for Push-ups

Propeller Stretch

Make large circles with arms from the shoulder joint moving them like dual propellers. After fifteen seconds, reverse direction of arms.

How to Use the Charts

The *Living Strength Ultimate Push-up Training System* has been created to give you a truly customized training regimen. It is a system unlike any other, in that it is based solely on you and your current strength and conditioning level. It allows you to advance as far as you wish in achieving superior strength and conditioning at your own pace. Just follow the instructions below for using the charts to your own best advantage.

STEP 1: Perform the Monday maximum test set using the Standard Military Push-up. Write that number down. It will be somewhere between 10 and 100 repetitions. This number represents your 100% best effort. If you can perform more than 100 repetitions of the Standard Military Push-up, you will then move up to one of the three more intense variations. If, on the other hand, you perform fewer than 10 repetitions, you will base your program on one of the three less intense variations. Whatever variation you choose must allow you to perform at least 10 repetitions minimum but less than 75 maximum. If you can perform 75 or more repetitions in your test set, then immediately move up to one of the three more intense variations.

STEP 2: Now, look at the charts. The percentages column begins on the far left at the top at 100% effort as represented by your test set maximum and then descends in the left column in increments all the way down to 20% at the bottom.

STEP 3: The column beginning at the immediate right of the 100% column represents the number you have performed in your maximum repetition test set. In other words, your 100% effort test set will be somewhere between 10 repetitions and 100 repetitions as indicated on the 100% line.

PERCENTAGE OF MAX REPETITIONS (performed hourly)	N U M B E R O			
100%	10	15	20	25
90%	9	14	18	23
85%	9	13	17	22
80%	8	12	16	20
75%	8	12	15	19
70%	7	11	14	18
65%	7	10	13	17
60%	6	9	12	15
55%	6	9	11	14
50%	5	8	10	13
45%	5	7	9	12
40%	4	6	8	10
35%	4	6	7	9
30%	3	5	6	8

PERCENTAGE OF MAX REPETITIONS *(performed hourly)*	NUMBER OF MAXIMUM								
100%	10	15	20	25	30	35	40	45	50
90%	9	14	18	23	27	32	36	41	45
85%	9	13	17	22	26	30	34	39	43
80%	8	12	16	20	24	28	32	36	40
75%	8	12	15	19	23	27	30	34	38
70%	7	11	14	18	21	25	28	32	35
65%	7	10	13	17	20	23	26	30	33
60%	6	9	12	15	18	21	24	27	30
55%	6	9	11	14	17	20	22	25	28
50%	5	8	10	13	15	18	20	23	25
45%	5	7	9	12	14	16	18	21	23
40%	4	6	8	10	12	14	16	18	20
35%	4	6	7	9	11	13	14	16	18
30%	3	5	6	8	9	11	12	14	15
25%	3	4	5	7	8	9	10	12	13
20%	2	3	4	5	6	7	8	9	10

CUSTOMIZED PUSH-

REPETITIONS *(from rep test set)*									
55	60	65	70	75	80	85	90	95	100
50	54	59	63	68	72	77	81	86	90
47	51	56	60	64	68	73	77	81	85
44	48	52	56	60	64	68	72	76	80
42	45	49	53	57	60	64	68	72	75
39	42	46	49	53	56	60	63	67	70
36	39	43	46	49	52	56	59	62	65
33	36	39	42	45	48	51	54	57	60
31	33	36	39	42	44	47	50	53	55
28	30	33	35	38	40	43	45	48	50
25	27	30	32	34	36	39	41	43	45
22	24	26	28	30	32	34	36	38	40
20	21	23	25	27	28	30	32	34	35
17	18	20	21	23	24	26	27	29	30
14	15	17	18	19	20	22	23	24	25
11	12	13	14	15	16	17	18	19	20

UP TRAINING CHART

STEP 4: The numbers on each subsequent horizontal line represent the corresponding percentage of each number in the top line. For example, let's say you performed 40 Standard Military Push-ups in good form. Find 40 repetitions on the 100% line at the top. Next, since your goal for the balance of Day 1 is to perform 35% of that number once every hour, you will follow 40 straight down to where that column intersects with the 35% column on the left side of the chart. In other words, you will be performing 14 repetitions every hour throughout the balance of the day and stop within 1 to 2 hours of bedtime. Now, let's say that you performed your first set at 7 a.m. and performed one set of 14 repetitions every hour thereafter until 9 p.m. That means a total of 14 sets of 14 repetitions = 196 repetitions + the original 40 repetition maximum test set for a grand total of 236 repetitions.

On Day 2, you would begin at 7 a.m. performing sets at 50% of max (20 push-ups) once every hour just as listed for Week One, Day 2. That means that by the end of the day you would have performed 12 to 15 sets total or somewhere between 240 and 300 repetitions. Your goal is to follow the charts each day, performing the percentages of maximum listed as well as the rest intervals listed between sets. Don't cheat. Obviously, real life sometimes gets in the way, and you might have to miss a few sets on any given day. What to do? Just get back on schedule as soon as you can. Don't lose your cool about a family or business obligation, don't do a set of push-ups during the middle of a movie in a crowded theater, and whatever you do, don't get upset about it. As Uncle Wally Nordkvist would say, *"Don't do or say something permanently stupid just because you are temporarily upset."* Needless to say, he was right.

PERCENTAGE OF MAX REPETITIONS (performed hourly)	NUMBER OF MAXIMU							
100%	10	15	20	25	30	35	40	45
90%	9	14	18	23	27	32	36	41
85%	9	13	17	22	26	30	34	39
80%	8	12	16	20	24	28	32	36
75%	8	12	15	19	23	27	30	34
70%	7	11	14	18	21	25	28	32
65%	7	10	13	17	20	23	26	30
60%	6	9	12	15	18	21	24	27
55%	6	9	11	14	17	20	22	25
50%	5	8	10	13	15	18	20	23
45%	5	7	9	12	14	16	18	21
40%	4	6	8	10	12	14	16	18
35%	4	6	7	9	11	13	**14**	16
30%	3	5	6	8	9	1	2	14

STEP 5: With the *Living Strength Ultimate Push-ups for the Awesome Physique* Training System, you will be training 7 days of each week. The levels of intensity as determined by the percentages of max as well as rest intervals between sets will vary from day to day, and it is this variance that Dr. Morehouse discovered was essential for achieving best possible results. Why? Because it is necessary to challenge yourself in order to create the need for adaptation; yet, at the same time, you want to be careful to not overtax your central nervous system. Hence the charts are exactly as Dr. Morehouse had determined for maximum efficiency.

STEP 6: Once you have accomplished your goal of 75 to 100 consecutive repetitions, you will be ready for any program in the entire *Living Strength Training System.* A good place to start is with the forthcoming *Living Strength Ultimate Ab Sculpting Training System.* This system of exercise will not only keep you lithe, lean, and sculpted, but it will also decompress your spine and keep you youthful and pain free for life.

STEP 7: Document your sets and repetitions daily.

LIVING STRENGTH™ DAILY PUSH-UPS

LIVING HEALTH, STRENGTH & FITNESS

WEEK: 1

	MON	TUE	WED	THU	FRI	SAT	SUN
%	35%	50%	60%	30%	50%	40%	25%
6AM	40 TEST						
7AM	14	20	24	12			
8AM	14	20	24	12			
9AM	14	20	24	12			
10AM	14	20	24	12			
11AM	14	20	24	12			
12PM	14	20	24	12			
1PM	14	20	24	12			
2PM	14	20	24				
3PM	14	20	24				
4PM	14	20	24				
5PM	14	20	24				
6PM	14	20	24				
7PM	14	20	24				
8PM	14	20	24				
9PM							
10PM							
TOTAL	40+196 (236)	280	336				

Push-up Program #2
Super Blitz Pyramid

As stated in *Program One,* I was a young martial arts instructor in 1977 when I first contacted Dr. Morehouse about his push-up program after having read his bestseller *Maximum Performance.* Over a period of several months I talked with him more than a dozen times, and we hit it off great. He said he enjoyed getting the feedback and photos of some of my best students in their *before* and *after* shots. Then six months after our first phone call, I called his office once again and asked his secretary, Angie, if I could speak with him. When she heard my voice, she was enthusiastic and said, "Hi, John. Just the other day Dr. Morehouse was asking me if I had heard from you. He'll be so glad to know that you've called again. Why don't you give me your number, and when he's out of his conference, he can give you a call."

I was a little taken back and asked, "Angie, are you serious? I know the doc is a busy man and maybe I should just call back another time."

She replied, "Don't you dare hang up without giving me your number, John."

"What do you mean?" I asked.

"I *mean* that Dr. Morehouse likes to talk with you," she stated, "and if you don't give me your number, I won't tell him you called."

That came as a real surprise. "All right, I got it, Angie." Needless to say, I was very pleased and gave her my number.

Sure enough, a few hours later I got a call from Doc Morehouse. The first thing he said was, "John, where have you been? I was beginning to wonder if you dropped off the face of the earth and we should send out a search party."

"Hey, Doc," I responded, laughing out loud, "you're a busy man, and I didn't want to bother you."

"I'd hardly consider a phone call from my favorite student a bother," he responded. "What can I help you with?"

Wow! I could hardly believe it. So I said, "Doc, your push-up program is the world's best, but you already know that, so that's a given. Still, there is one issue that some of my students are having to deal with."

"And what might that be?"

"Well, it's like this," I answered. "It's the end of October, and it's gettin' cold outside, which means before long there will be snow on the ground, and some of my students who are cops won't be able to pull over and do a quick set of push-ups in the park every hour. Some of them are wondering what Dr. Morehouse would recommend they should do?"

Without missing a beat, he said, "Tell your students that Dr. Morehouse recommends they do pyramids twice a day, morning and night."

That was certainly the straightforward answer I was hoping to hear. "Doc, could you give me the specifics of how that would look on paper?"

Dr. Laurence E. Morehouse then laid out the following pyramid training system complete with four weeks of charts. As was true of the original program, this pyramid training system has its origin in Dr. Morehouse alone and no one else.

Ultimate Push-ups Program Two: The Super Blitz Pyramid

STEP 1: Once again, our program starts on Monday morning with a "Test Set," and you will be using the same charts found on pages 80-81 to chart your progress. Dr. Morehouse was adamant that in order for any program to be effective the participants need to have "a frame of reference." In other words, it is essential to know where you were when you began and then to periodically test yourself in order to know where you are regarding your rate of progress and to make whatever adjustments are needed. So your first order of business is to drop down and take your test set in as close to perfect form as you can and write that number down. OK, have you done it? Good. Write it down here _______.

STEP 2: Next, for Week One you will perform pyramid sets Monday through Saturday, morning and evening (if you feel up to it). If you are just breaking in, for Week One you will perform five pyramid sets; if you are already in good shape, perform seven sets. So let's say 40 reps is your hypothetical test set maximum. If you are just breaking in, Dr. Morehouse stated that you would perform a pyramid set beginning at 30% of max and peaking at 50% in 10% increments of max for a total of five sets. In other words, using 40 reps as your test set max, you would do **12+16+20+16+12 = 76 reps** for the morning pyramid, and the same sequence in the evening for a total of 152 reps for the day. Between sets you will stand up, walk around the room, and practice deep costal breathing while moving your arms through a very light circular motion from the shoulders to keep the joints lubricated. Then as soon as you feel capable of your next set, drop down and do it and continue until you have performed all five sets.

If you are already in great shape, Doc Morehouse said, "Guys who are already in good shape can step it up a bit and do seven sets." In this case that means you would pyramid from 30% to 60% in increments of 10%. On paper, with 40 reps as your test set max, it would look like this: **12+16+20+24+20+16+12 = 120 reps x 2 (AM and PM) = 240 REPS**.

NOTE: as was true of *Program One*, with *Program Two* you will never approach your maximum on any given set, but you will achieve a high level cumulative total for the day. And as you will see on Week Two, when you perform your Monday morning test set the results are amazing. Then for weeks two through four you will perform the following morning and evening pyramid sequences.

STEP 3: Use this customized program for a total of 4 weeks. At the end of 4 weeks you can take on another more intense variation and start over at Week One or stay with the variation you like best and continue with Week Four as your guideline. This brings up a point. The Wednesday percentages of **60% + 70% + 80% + 90% + 80% + 70% + 60% x 2** are followed by Thursday's **30% + 40% + 50% + 60% + 50% + 40% + 30% x 2**. That is not a misprint. You'll know why once you're in Week Four.

DAY OF WEEK	WEEK TWO - PROGRAM 2: SUPER BLITZ PYRAMID								
	MON	30% +	40% +	50% +	60% +	50% +	40% +	30%	x 2
	TUE	40% +	50% +	60% +	70% +	60% +	50% +	40%	x 2
	WED	30% +	40% +	50% +	60% +	50% +	40% +	30%	x 2
	THUR	40% +	50% +	60% +	70% +	60% +	50% +	40%	x 2
	FRI	30% +	40% +	50% +	60% +	50% +	40% +	30%	x 2
	SAT	40% +	50% +	60% +	70% +	60% +	50% +	40%	x 2
	SUN	Take the day off							

Once again, for week two we are using **40 REPS** as our frame of reference.
MONDAY: 12+16+20+24+20+16+12 = 120 reps x 2 = **240 REPS**
TUESDAY: 16+20+24+28+24+20+16 = 148 reps x 2 = **296 REPS**

DAY OF WEEK	WEEK THREE - PROGRAM 2: SUPER BLITZ PYRAMID								
	MON	30% +	40% +	50% +	60% +	50% +	40% +	30%	x 2
	TUE	40% +	50% +	60% +	70% +	60% +	50% +	40%	x 2
	WED	50% +	60% +	70% +	80% +	70% +	60% +	50%	x 2
	THUR	30% +	40% +	50% +	60% +	50% +	40% +	30%	x 2
	FRI	40% +	50% +	60% +	70% +	60% +	50% +	40%	x 2
	SAT	50% +	60% +	70% +	80% +	70% +	60% +	50%	x 2
	SUN	Take the day off							

DAY OF WEEK	WEEK FOUR - PROGRAM 2: SUPER BLITZ PYRAMID								
	MON	40% +	50% +	60% +	70% +	60% +	50% +	40%	x 2
	TUE	30% +	40% +	50% +	60% +	50% +	40% +	30%	x 2
	WED	60% +	70% +	80% +	90% +	80% +	70% +	60%	x 2
	THUR	30% +	40% +	50% +	60% +	50% +	40% +	30%	x 2
	FRI	40% +	50% +	60% +	70% +	60% +	50% +	40%	x 2
	SAT	50% +	60% +	70% +	80% +	70% +	60% +	50%	x 2
	SUN	Take the day off							

NOTE: Between *Programs One* and *Two* you have everything required to achieve push-up mastery and an awesome physique. Both programs yield equal results. Granted Program Two is tougher than Program One due to the volume that you will perform in two condensed workouts. But after a month on this program the only thing you'll be complaining about is the new shirts you'll have to buy because your arms, chest, shoulders, and upper back have outgrown your old ones. But then again, there are worse problems for a man to deal with.

Push-up Variations

The seven push-up variations pictured here allow for steady and progressive increases in dynamic athletic strength and superior muscular development. Start wherever you are and follow the charts exactly as outlined before moving to the next higher level of intensity. When you get to the point that you can perform 100 consecutive repetitions of variation #7: The Living Strength Push-up, you will have achieved a level of extraordinary athletic strength, fitness, and physique that very few men ever achieve.

#1 Counter Assist
(Ron Watson Special)

#2 Knee Assist

#3 Atlas I

#4 Military

#5 Atlas II

#6 Jack King

#7 Living Strength

chapter FOUR

nutrition

Fast Recovery Nutrition

"Nothing will benefit human health and increase the chances for survival of life on Earth as much as the evolution to a vegetarian. Vegetarian food leaves a deep impression on our nature. If the whole world adopts vegetarianism, it can change the destiny of humankind."

Albert Einstein

Fast Recovery Nutrition

In order to achieve the best possible results from *Living Strength Ultimate Push-ups for the Awesome Physique*, you'll need to feed your body the best possible nutrition to fuel your workouts and rebuild your muscles and nerves in world-record time. No exceptions! The good news is you're in luck, because that is exactly what this next chapter is all about, and truth to tell, no one whom I have ever met knows more about super fast recovery than my friend Rod Fisher. He knows because he has done it! Rod was a champion gymnast who set records at his high school for pull-ups and the rope climb that still stand to this day more than 50 years later. And today, in his mid 60s, Rod still has the kind of rock hard physique and

muscularity that the vast majority of men one-third his age wish they had.

How did he do it? Pay attention, kemosabe, because Rod will share some of his secrets in this chapter. In fact, by following Rod's advice, you'll experience four almost magical things simultaneously: (1) Your energy, including your ability to think and concentrate will go through the roof. (2) You will feel your strength, endurance, and muscle and nerve force surge as never before. (3) Your basal metabolic rate will be so heightened that you will immediately start losing unnecessary body fat. And most important, (4) you'll start to feel good all the time as aches and pains become a distant memory and your sleep becomes restful and restorative. With all the above said, here's Rod Fisher.

Vegan-Powered Nutrition for Super-Charged Strength and Healing

As an athlete, you want to channel the greatest possible amount of energy toward peak performance and have enough energy left over for recovery. Getting the right nutrients is absolutely essential to accomplishing that goal, and yet very few athletes give adequate thought to what kind of fuel will really enhance their performance. They know about carbo-loading and protein powders and drinking water, but most simply fill up on whatever they want. The problem is that this "whatever" they're consuming can impede recovery by forcing the body to divert energy away from muscle repair to digestion. When that happens, muscle building is s-l-o-w-e-d down tremendously. It doesn't have to be like that. What to do? Use your head and embrace fast recovery vegan-powered nutrition.

Think about this: the biggest stress we have on our bodies, the biggest consumer of our energy, is *nutritional stress*. When you eat foods that are easily digestible, it maximizes efficient digestion and the assimilation of nutrients and eliminates excess work and stress for the body. In other words, it makes you feel energized instead of feeling as though you need to take a long nap. It only makes sense that by embracing fast recovery nutrition that you'll have more energy sooner for exercise, and you'll be able to increase the pace of your training regimen and build more muscle faster. This is essential because with our *Ultimate Push-ups for the Awesome Physique Program*, we promote daily exercise and not every other day. Why? Because correctly applied daily training with properly applied speed recovery plant nutrition will infuse your muscles with highly oxygenated blood complete with growth factors and deliver vastly superior results. You will be able to get in more workouts and therefore get stronger and fitter faster, provided you embrace fast recovery vegan nutrition. Believe me, I know from experience.

The opposite is equally true. For instance, a high fat, high protein diet will increase the uric acid level in your bloodstream and have a detrimental effect on your joints and on the muscles themselves. You will feel like Super Man in a room full of kryptonite. You'll feel fatigued and sore all the time as well as crave sugars and starches, which will diminish your ability to work out as well as recover. Furthermore, if your diet is laden with processed and chemically altered foods, your body cannot recognize them, so it has to work overtime to digest and assimilate whatever nutrients it may have, which depletes your energy reserves even further.

In my book *Living Strength: The Vegan Way to Super Health, Strength, Fitness & Healing,* we set forth the cornerstone truth that a natural diet comprised of vegetables (especially leafy greens), raw fruits, seeds, and nuts is the way we used to eat, the way we were meant to eat, and the way we should all eat now. Nature intended for us to get our nutrients from real food, not pills or powders or processed and engineered foods, and it's still the very best, most effective, most efficient, most delicious, and most satisfying way to get the appropriate balance of vital nutrients. If you are eating these whole, plant-based alkaline-forming foods that are easily digestible, nutrient dense, and highly bioavailable, you will reduce the stress of digestion upon your body and aid the assimilation and use of the nutrients.

One of the first things I do in *The Vegan Way* is to debunk the myths that have traditionally caused people to shy away from a natural diet. Take, for instance, the multitude of myths surrounding protein, particularly how much we need and the best places to get it. The truth is that if you

eat a natural diet, with a good variety of vegetables and fruits enhanced with 2-4 ounces of seeds and nuts, you will get all the protein your body needs to live in a state of super health, strength, and fitness, and you will also heal and recover in world-record time. Balance and variety are the golden keys to a healthy diet.

Here are the straight facts regarding protein: (1) Overconsumption of animal-based protein can damage long-term health by poisoning the liver and kidneys and elevating uric acid levels in the bloodstream to the point that uric acid crystals begin to form and accumulate in one's joints. This, in turn, causes an extremely painful arthritic condition referred to as gout. If you have not experienced gout, count yourself fortunate because we're told that those who have experienced it never want to experience it again. The best way to avoid gout and other painful arthritic conditions, as well as protect your liver and kidneys so that you won't end up needing dialysis three times each week, is to eliminate all animal-based protein from your diet (including dairy products) and switch to plant-based protein that improves not only your performance but dramatically increases your prospects for long-term, pain-free super health. (2) We need much less protein than we think we do. The idea that athletes need 1 gram of protein for each pound of body weight daily is ludicrous. FACT: a growing minority of the world's greatest athletes who participate in some of the world's most grueling and demanding sports, such as Iron Man triathlons and mixed martial arts, are vegans who consume 1 gram of protein per kilogram (2.2 pounds) of body weight daily. They recover faster and perform at a much higher standard than non-vegan athletes. (3) We can get all the protein we need from a plant-based diet that includes generous amounts of seeds, nuts, leafy greens, brocolli, quinoa, buckwheat, spirulina, and chlorella.

I also will give you the straight scoop on fat. Did you know that the best sources of essential fatty acids are raw seeds and nuts, which include raw seed and nut butters? Monounsaturated fat from seeds, nuts, and vegetables are excellent sources of EFAs. You don't have to be afraid of these excellent sources of *essential fatty acids* because, after all, they are *essential* for achieving and maintaining super health and fitness. However, saturated fat from meat and dairy clogs arteries, promotes heart disease, causes high blood pressure, and creates kidney stones, not to mention a whole host of other debilitating health problems, including gout and arthritis.

I also clue you in on what food combining is all about as well as the simple dynamics of eating raw, juicing, and blending? The goal is, very simply, to help your body digest food as efficiently and quickly as possible. If your body is not taxed with the hard work of digesting food, that extra energy that it's not exerting in the digestive process means more energy for recovery, repair, and enhanced performance. Athletes can apply that extra energy to their workouts or to the recovery period after their workout (therefore enabling them to train more frequently and intensively). And even nonathletes will enjoy greater clarity of mind, increased vigor, and fewer dips in energy.

Keep in mind that when you exercise, you are breaking down muscle cells, which is a good and complementary stress. Muscles store glycogen, which is basically the way the body stores glucose. Our muscles burn that glycogen as fuel during a workout. After a workout, the body is depleted of glycogen and needs to restore its supply as quickly as possible, in order to be ready for the next burst of exercise. *The Vegan Way* delivers superior nutrition to rebuild those cells with the proper building blocks that are delivered via the bloodstream. If you practice FIT (F-Frequent I-Interval T-Training) throughout the day, you're going to be delivering highly oxygenated blood with all the nutrition and growth factors to the muscles, causing quicker rebuilding and the cell structures become much stronger as a result. Better nutrition creates a stronger body, and therefore fuels better exercise performance and a speedier recovery, which is precisely what you want.

We can make you one promise: *If you adopt any part of this vegan lifestyle, you will feel healthier, stronger, and more energetic than you currently do.* And if you are an athlete, you will be better able to reach your potential and recover more quickly. To optimize the benefits, adopt all parts of the lifestyle immediately. Nutrition and exercise are inextricably linked, and each enhances the beneficial effects of the other. We think it's fair to say that *plant-powered nutrition and body-weight strength exercises are the keys to the fountain of youth.*

The Optimal Post Workout Meal

If you are performing a major workout along with this push-up regimen, as the optimal post workout meal (eat within 45 minutes), we highly recommend you consider doing what we do by making a vegetable juice with lots of leafy greens, carrots and/or beets, and ginger, or a fruit smoothie with some celery, sea vegetables, and leafy greens in it. It takes just a few minutes, contains all the recovery factors needed, gives us a good dose of the right nutrients, and tastes absolutely delicious. For instance, we'll throw in whatever fruit is in season, some lettuce, kale collard leaves, a stalk or two of celery, and sea vegetables and blend them all together. The leafy greens add minerals, and the celery and sea vegetables add sodium, which is another key nutrient after a workout (when we've lost sodium through our sweat).

Other times, we just throw several bananas into a blender with some water and make a very simple smoothie from that. We occasionally throw in some grapes for added juiciness, maybe some leafy greens, or a bit of spirulina and chlorella for added protein. Because of the fiber in the fruit and leafy greens, my blood sugar levels rise at exactly the proper rate to be absorbed by my body. And since the

blender breaks down the food's cell walls, a lot of the preliminary work of digesting the ingredients has already been done. The smoothie doesn't require as much energy to digest as those fruits and greens would if eaten in whole form.

Sometimes I crave a monomeal, which means that I eat only one kind of food for the entire meal. After an especially intense workout, I've been known to eat up to six bananas or oranges. This may sound like a lot, but consuming a single food is much easier on the body and doesn't tax your digestion. So it's much like eating a smoothie. Listen to your body and don't hesitate to give it what it is craving. It's working hard to restore itself as quickly as possible. The main point with all of these options is that you want to get these essential nutrients into your body quickly, and you don't want to stress your body and digestive process with a lot of other kinds of food that it doesn't want and doesn't need but would have to digest and eliminate.

This is all another way of saying that *the last thing you should do after a big workout is to sit down and indulge in a high fat, high complex-carb meal, such as beer and pizza.* Doing so just means you're taxing your body doubly: It is trying to recover from your workout *and* diverting energy to digestion at the same time. In addition to that, high fat foods slow down the rate of absorption of glucose into the bloodstream. So your muscles aren't getting those much-needed replenishments when they need them most. You also don't need a lot of protein right after working out. Protein is not a fuel and takes more work to be digested and assimilated. While your muscles do need protein for muscle repair, high quantities of protein are not the ideal food right after a workout. Some seeds/nuts and leafy greens two hours after a fruit meal are great. I've heard that digestion of a particularly heavy meal takes more energy than running a marathon. That makes sense when you consider that several famous people in history have died of a coronary immediately after eating a heavy meal. *So if you want to recover quickly and kick up your training a notch, stay away from the foods that take a lot of time, effort, and stress to digest.*

If you plan to be working out for a long time (over an hour), it's a good idea to replenish those glycogen reserves sometime *during* your workout. I often consume an orange or two during my longer workouts (over an hour) just to keep my energy up. Fruit is ideal because it is easy to digest and contains both glucose and fructose. The fructose gives me an immediate kick start and the glucose supplies my body with a slower, more sustained energy boost. That means I can work out harder and longer than if I waited until the end of my routine to eat.

You also want to get hydrated quickly after a workout. The good news is that if you eat a lot of fruit (either whole or in a smoothie), you'll be getting plenty of water through that, which brings up an important point: a cooked meal is dehydrating and will tap whatever liquid reserves you have left. So stay away from foods that have the water cooked out of them.

If you follow this regimen, you'll also enjoy another side benefit—fewer injuries. Your body will be better able to repair muscle tissue and therefore be better up to the task of performing as your training sessions become more frequent and rigorous.

Now let me address another issue. Oftentimes the unitiated assume that adopting a vegan lifestyle means that they will be living a very limited lifestyle of privation and deprivation, and nothing could be further from the truth. In fact, the exact opposite is true. You will be feasting every day on a wide variety of delicious and nourishing foods that will make every cell in your body feel alive. Consider the following.

Vegan-Powered Nutrition

If you are skeptical as to whether a natural diet is delicious as well as sustainable, here are some examples of how to eat right the vegan way and love it: (courtesy of Ecopolitan Restaurant, Minneapolis, MN)

Purple Kale Salad—kale, red cabbage, tomato, kiwi, fresh basil, raisins, tahini-garlic dressing

Taco Salad—baby greens, lentil taco meat, bell pepper, tomato, avocado, onion, olives, cilantro, hot sauce, cashew sour cream, avocado dressing

Mediterranean Salad—spinach, cucumber, tomato, olives, cashew parmesan, hummus, cherry vinaigrette, served with flax crackers

Garlic Avocado Salad—kale, avocado, red onion, tomato, garlic vinaigrette

Sweet Spinach Salad—spinach, oranges, red onion, strawberries, sunflower seeds, pecans, cherry vinaigrette

Mock Tuna Crisps—walnut faux tuna on flaxseed-sunflower shells with baby greens, tomato, red onion, mustard

Savory Casserole—dill cashew cheese, fresh vegetables layered with zucchini, avocado, buckwheat bread crumbs, served with a side salad

Macaroni and Cheese—zucchini noodles and a creamy cashew cheese topped with tomato, fresh herbs, scallions, cashew parmesan, served on a bed of spinach

Flaxseed Tostadas—two flax seed-sunflower shells with lentil taco meat, greens, marinated mushrooms, onions, olives, cilantro, cashew sour cream, hot sauce, served with salsa, guacamole

Ginger Nut Noodles—peanut-style ginger sauce made with Brazil nuts on zucchini, carrot, daikon noodles with basil, cilantro, scallions, cucumber, served on house-dressed greens

Chili Cheese Burrito—a collard leaf wrap with lentil taco meat, fresh vegetables, nacho cheese, sunflower seeds, sprouts, sour cream, hot sauce, served with salsa, guacamole

Falafel Wrap—a collard leaf wrap with hummus, falafel, cucumber, tomato, olives, sprouts, tahini-garlic dressing, served with a side salad

Nachos Supreme—cashew nacho cheese on kale with bell pepper, cucumber, marinated mushrooms, red onion, cilantro, olives, cashew sour cream, hot sauce, served with eco chips

Marinara Pasta—sweet sundried tomato marinara sauce on zucchini noodles with strawberries, red onion, olives, fresh herbs, cherry reduction, served on cherry vinaigrette-dressed spinach

Pesto Pasta—pesto sauce on zucchini noodles with tomato, bell pepper, marinated mushrooms, walnuts, served on cherry vinaigrette-dressed spinach.

As you can see from the list of salads and entrees, vegan food is anything but tasteless and boring. It is, in fact, the most delicious, satisfying, and nutritious food you can possibly eat. But even more important is the fact that as you transition to a vegan lifestyle, your body will become much stronger and healthier as a direct result. Granted, the idea of becoming totally vegan may seem foreign to some men, but the good news is that as you begin to see and feel the difference, you will be motivated not only to continue this way of eating, but to move up to a 100% plant-based diet. If you are still unconvinced, let me ask you the following question.

What Would You Rather Have?

From time to time, I come across people who know nothing about a vegan lifestyle, and the first thing they tell me is, "I could never do that." My response is always respectful, but I contrast their "I could never do that" statements by asking them the following "Would you rather" questions.

- **Would you rather** live, look, and feel younger than your years or die from an easily preventable disease years ahead of your true potential?
- **Would you rather** be sitting on the sidelines of life because you're too fat and tired or have an abundance of energy and exuberance for living that never tires?

- **Would you rather** be overweight and out of shape or have a lithe, lean sculpted body that not only "feels good" but one that you feel good about 24/7?
- **Would you rather** have high cholesterol, hypertension, and heart disease or have the heart and lungs of an Olympic athlete?
- **Would you rather** have prostate, breast, colon, or other cancers or remain cancer free your entire life?
- **Would you rather** have diabetes and kidney disease that requires dialysis or prevent either from ever happening?
- **Would you rather** be taking expensive medications to mask the pain of gout and swollen arthritic joints or have strong, athletic, pain-free joints for life?
- **Would you rather** have Alzheimer's disease or remain clearheaded and sharp until the day you die?

Closing Thoughts and a Preview from *The Vegan Way*

It all comes down to this. You have a choice in life. You can sputter and stumble and creak your way along in a process of slow, painful decline—or you can take charge of your health destiny and become a human dynamo. The choice is yours! If you choose to become the dynamo that you can be, there is no better way to achieve the lasting benefits of super health, strength, fitness, and healing than to embrace the entire *Living Strength Training System of Natural Physical Culture.* You have just completed Course One—*Ultimate Push-Ups for the Awesome Physique*—that outlines and underscores the single most important foundational exercise in the entire realm of Physical Culture for creating both functional and foundational strength and fitness for life. You have also

been introduced to the benefits of vegan-powered nutrition for super fast recovery and healing. With the above in mind, I'd like to present the following excerpt from: *Living Strength: The Vegan Way to Super Health, Strength, Fitness, & Healing.* I'm doing this because it underscores the difference that superior, plant-based vegan nutrition can make in optimizing your performance and accelerating muscle recovery between bouts of the most strenuous and intense exercise that a human being can do. It is, in fact, part of my story—the part that my friend John Peterson was referring to in introducing this chapter when he stated: "In order to achieve the best possible results from *Living Strength Ultimate Push-ups for the Awesome Physique*, you'll need to feed your body the best possible nutrition to fuel your workouts and rebuild your muscles and nerves in world-record time. No exceptions!"

I hope you enjoy the following excerpt from *Living Strength: The Vegan Way to Super Health, Strength, Fitness, & Healing.*

The Super F.I.T. Method

TO SUPER SPORTS PERFORMANCE

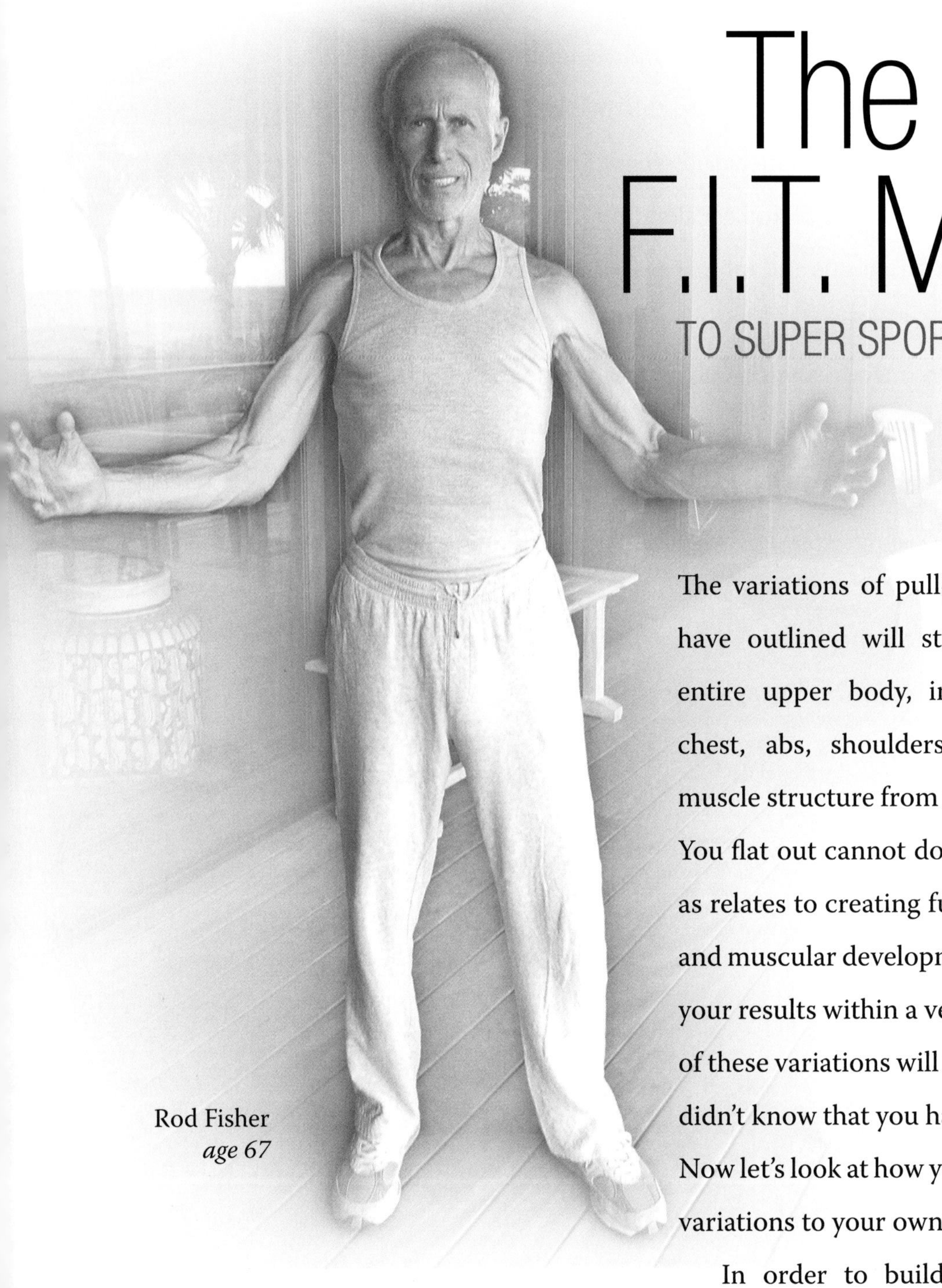

Rod Fisher
age 67

The variations of pull-ups and chin-ups that we have outlined will strengthen and sculpt your entire upper body, including forearms, biceps, chest, abs, shoulders, and entire upper back muscle structure from all angles and all directions. You flat out cannot do better than these exercises as relates to creating functional full body strength and muscular development as will be obvious from your results within a very short time. In fact, some of these variations will make you sore in places you didn't know that you had *places*, let alone muscles. Now let's look at how you can utilize these multiple variations to your own best advantage.

In order to build your functional strength as quickly as possible and to transform your musculature in world-record time, we utilize two methods of training. For beginners, the first is the more important of the two, because it builds foundational strength very quickly and safely and is based on the *Frequent Interval Training* method that was first developed and refined by physiologist Dr. Laurence E. Morehouse of the UCLA Human Performance Laboratory when he was working with America's astronauts in the early 1960s. Dr. Morehouse's goal was to transform America's astronauts as quickly as possible into some of the world's strongest and fittest men, so they could withstand the rigors of the space program while minimizing the devastating physiological effects of zero gravity. He experimented with every known exercise modality until he developed *Frequent Interval Training* and eureka! He nailed it! This method was so successful that it was soon used by Olympic trainers and has been in use by Olympic athletes and coaches worldwide since that time as part of the standard training protocol.

This is the same training method Rod and I call, "Greasing the Groove." And it is literally the same training protocol Rod used to turn himself into a champion gymnast in high school. In fact, because of the strength he developed by utilizing the Greasing the Groove training method, in 1964 Rod set a record in a high school gymnastics meet of 3.5 seconds in the rope climb that still stands today—nearly 50 years after he set it!

So what exactly is the Greasing the Groove training method? In a nutshell, it's training in sub-maximal sets throughout the entire day. Here's Rod's story in his own words.

As a kid growing up in New York City, I loved to go to the movies, and there was one movie in particular that had a profound impact on me and was instrumental in me becoming a gymnast. In 1956, when I was ten years old, my mom and dad took my sister and me to see Trapeze, *starring Burt Lancaster, Tony Curtis, and Gina Lollobrigida. Unlike the movies of today,* Trapeze *was not a showcase of special effects—not by a long shot. It instead showcased the very real physical talents of the actors. To this day, I haven't seen actors in better shape than Burt Lancaster and Tony Curtis were in when they made* Trapeze. *Both men had an ultra lean, lithe, muscular development that was totally functional. As a result of the training regimen that they both followed, neither man had an ounce of unnecessary weight and were totally believable as they made climbing the rope to the trapeze look like child's play. Another reason it was so believable was that before he became a movie actor, Lancaster was a circus aerialist doing exactly what he did in* Trapeze.

From that time on I was destined to be a gymnast, and I taught myself how to walk on my hands just like Tony Curtis and Burt Lancaster did in Trapeze. *When I got to junior high, I often walked around the gymnasium on my hands, and even though we didn't have gymnastics as an official sport at my junior high, I was always practicing it. That paid off handsomely because as a wrestler, I never once met anyone in my weight class who was nearly as strong as I was from my gymnastics training. In fact, from seventh through ninth grade I thrived as a wrestler and had an incredible winning streak. I would have stuck with wrestling, but as luck would have it, when I became a junior at Oceanside High School in 1963, we had our first gymnastics team. I specialized on the rope climb and the high bar.*

In the rope climb, a contestant starts in an L-Sit position on the floor, climbs the 20-foot long rope, and must touch a tambourine at the top that is charcoaled in order to prove you completed the climb. And, yes, they check your hands for proof. Once you start from the L-Sit position, no part of your body can touch the floor—not even slightly. If it does, you are disqualified.

From day one, I trained hard and did everything the coaches asked of me and more. Finally, when we had our big meet, I faced off against a young man named Mark Breslin who was an extraordinary athlete, and he beat me decisively. Naturally, my teammates tried to make me feel better by telling me that I did fantastic, considering I outweighed him by a good 30 pounds. But I wasn't interested in excuses. Breslin beat me because he had a near flawless technique with no wasted effort. So I went to his school a few times to watch him train. Frankly, I marveled at the precision of his movements and could hardly believe what I saw. I made mental notes and then began to apply what I had learned, making necessary adjustments in my technique to match my own body. I improved dramatically, but my time still was not as fast as his.

Finally, it dawned on me that I needed to be much stronger if I was going to have a shot at beating Breslin. So I decided I was going to do something I had never heard of anyone attempting, let alone doing—1,000 pull-ups a day every other day. Why 1,000? Because even though I outweighed Breslin by 30 pounds, I made a commitment to myself that if he beat me again, it would not be because he was stronger. No way! So I got to work and put together a strategy to perform 1,000 pull-ups every other day. That meant that I began knocking off sets of 20 to 25 or sometimes even 30 pull-ups throughout the entire day from early morning to just before bed until I did at least 1,000 pull-ups. It also meant that some days I did well over 40 sets. I got to a point where I could knock out 42 consecutive pull-ups in a single set. As you might imagine, my strength and endurance went through the roof. And I knew that the next time I met Breslin I would be ready.

When summer came, to get some spending money I got an ushers' job at the local theater. Within a few a days I was enjoying my job and my new friends, but I couldn't find a place to chin myself. After word got out to the other ushers that I was a gymnast and performed 1,000 chins every other day, one of my usher friends warned me that one of the other ushers who was about 6'4" and weighed about 240 pounds was jealous of me. My friend said, "Rod, you gotta be careful because that guy has it in for you, and I think he's going to try to push you into a fight." I thanked him and pretended to take his caution seriously, but on the inside I was laughing because I had grown up in a part of New York City where self-defense was something you did for survival, and I was very good at survival.

Later that same night, four of us ushers, including the big guy, were taking a break before the next show let out. I looked him over closely, and it was obvious that he was a weightlifter. While we were talking, my friend pointed to a slight ledge on a door molding just above the door and said, "Hey, Rod, I wonder if anyone could do a pull-up hanging from there? It would probably be impossible." One by one they all tried, but none of them could even hang from the molding, because there was only enough room for the very tips of the fingers halfway up to the first knuckle. Then it hit me—that's where I'll do my chins! I went over and grabbed the molding. Uncomfortable? Yes, but not too bad. So I started knocking off pull-ups and stopped at 30 in a row. When I turned around, everyone was staring in awe. Even the big guy was impressed, and from that moment on we became friends and he was always talking about how strong I was.

Several months later, the new gymnastics season was underway and the day came when I met up with Mark Breslin. In addition to being in the best shape of my life, I was also adrenalized to the max, and this time the outcome was totally different. Afterward, he came over to congratulate me and said, "I can't believe what you just did." To which I responded, "Now you know how I felt last time." We shook hands, and he said, "Next time." We met up again, but "next time" never happened. My secret was my pull-ups. I was Greasing the Groove every chance I had, and it paid off."

Okay, let's review. Greasing the Groove or *Frequent Interval Training* is the superior training method for increasing muscular strength and endurance as fast as is humanly possible. It allows one to perform an incredible volume of training without depleting or overtaxing your central nervous system. This is due to the fact that you have long rest periods between sets and your muscles are always fresh. In addition, you never push your muscles to perform more than 75% of your maximum in any given set. In fact, generally speaking you will want to keep your repetitions in the 50–70% range. This is truly custom designing your workout to meet your individual, very specific needs and abilities.

So, *how do you know what 50–70% of your maximum rep range is?* Answer: You test yourself first thing every Monday morning. For your test, you will use the Classic Pull-Up. So go to your bar, jump up, and perform one set in good form until you feel you are within one rep of failure and then stop. Write that number down. Let's say you are in great shape and did 9 reps. That means for the balance of the day you will perform 5 pull-ups (55% of max) at least once every hour for the balance of the day. In 12 hours, that means you will be doing at least 60 pull-ups. Then on Wednesday, you would perform 6 reps (66% of max) at least once every hour for a total of 72 reps. On Friday, you push just a little harder and perform sets of 7 reps, but you will give yourself up to 90 minutes between sets. You would then rest completely on Saturday and Sunday and test yourself again the following Monday. This time it would not be the least bit unusual if your max increased by 2 to 3 reps. Naturally, you would write that number down and base all of your sets throughout the day on your new maximum number. Before long you'll be doubling the number of reps you did in your first test set, and at that point you may decide to do sets more frequently than just once each hour. That's up to you. In time you will know intuitively how many and how often. You'll discover that at the beginning, there is no better way to build volume as well as supercharged strength and endurance than by Greasing the Groove.

So what are you waiting for? Get to work.

The Pyramid Set System of Training

Once you have mastered Greasing the Groove, you will be ready for *Pyramid Set Training.* Both methods are incredibly effective, but Greasing the Groove (G-T-G) is the superior of the two for increasing beginning stage strength. However, once you are satisfied with your strength, you may want to include more variations from more angles to maximize your development, and for that we will use Pyramid Set Training. This is the best and quickest way to build both muscular strength and endurance. We call it Pyramid Training because it utilizes a series of ascending repetitions followed by a corresponding series of descending repetitions.

Let's say, for example, that in week one you have already built your base with G-T-G, but now you are willing to push yourself exceptionally hard to take it over the top and achieve sensational results in both strength and development. For week one you will do the following.

The Classic Pull-up

Let's just say that at the moment you can perform 12 Classic Pull-ups (that would be exceptional for most men, by the way) in good form before reaching failure. Let's also say that your goal is get to the point of performing 20 repetitions with no more difficulty than performing 12 at the present time. To achieve this, you will perform ascending sets beginning around 30% of max and continuing until you reach around 70% of max and then perform corresponding descending sets. This is how it would look on paper.

3+4+5+6+7+8+7+6+5+4+3 = 58 REPS

NOTE: You never push to the edge while building your foundation for future super performance and volume. In spite of not pushing to the edge of the edge, you still achieve a high number of repetitions, or *volume.* As your strength and conditioning improves, you will minimize the time of rest between sets as both your strength and endurance skyrocket. This is not just a conjecture on my part. It's a reality I have witnessed many, many times. In fact, I recommend that you retest yourself every sixth or seventh workout so you can readjust your repetitions to match your increase in strength and endurance. For example, let's say that today you can perform 12 reps in good form without performing the last one totally on your nerve force. Five workouts from now you should not be surprised if you can perform 13 repetitions in good form before you begin to overstress your CNS. At that point, we will reset the pyramid as follows.

4+5+6+7+8+9+8+7+6+5+4 = 69 REPS

Five workouts later, you will retest once again. At this point, 14 or 15 reps are very likely. This is how your new pyramid would look based on 30% on the low end to 70% on the high end,

5+6+7+8+9+10+11+10+9+8+7+6+5 = 101 REPS

From this point forward you can start adding other pyramid variations, performing the same sequence of 30% on the low end up to 70–75% percent on the high end. When you do, I recommend that you perform up to 3 or 4 pyramids in one workout, but absolutely never more than 5 in any given workout until you have reached your highest level of strength and fitness. Then you might be able to perform 6 complete pyramid circuits without CNS burnout. I also recommend that once you are doing 3 or more pyramid variations with 12 repetitions or more at the 70% peak of your pyramid, you then start performing your pyramid sets in increments of 2 instead of 1.

This is an example of what I am talking about. Let's say you can perform 16 reps on your test set in perfect form. Your pyramid would then be as follows:

6+8+10+12+10+8+6 = 60 REPS

Once you are strong enough to perform the sequence above, you can then add other variations. The more variations, the more

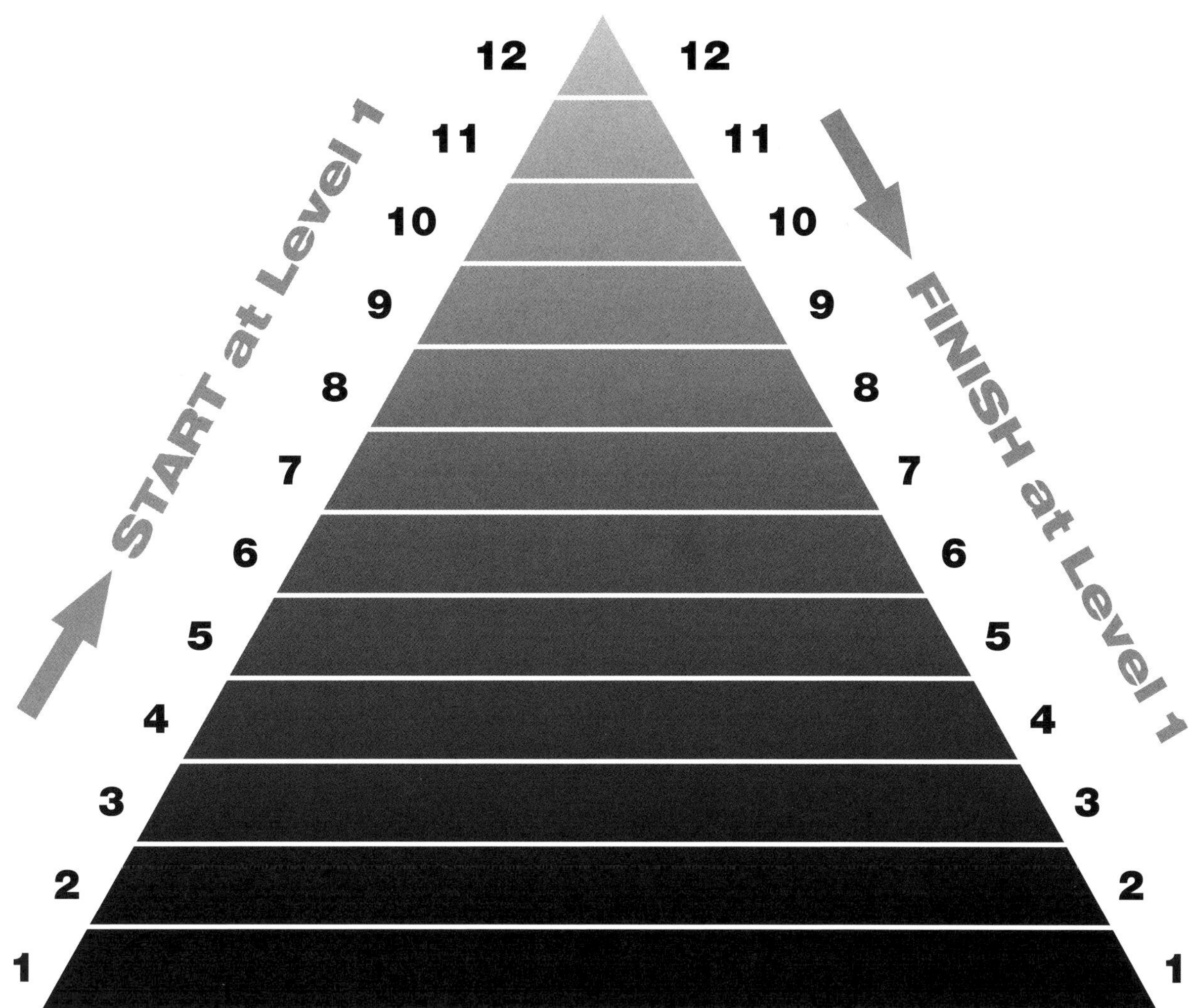

NOTE: The level you **max out at** - use as your benchmark and **then go back down the pyramid**.

reps you will total. A total of six pyramids in a workout with the sequence listed above would equate to 360 repetitions total. Here is a breakdown showing the number of pyramids and the total number of reps they equate to:

x **2** pyramid variations = **120 reps**
x **3** pyramid variations = **180 reps**
x **4** pyramid variations = **240 reps**
x **5** pyramid variations = **300 reps**
x **6** pyramid variations = **360 reps**

Once you have built your foundational strength and endurance utilizing the pyramid system outlined above, you will be able to move into high volume sets of 20 repetitions or more and perform up to 12 sets total. When you get into the really high numbers, you need to be sure that your muscles are doing the work and that you are not overtaxing your joints and connective tissues as the result of using poor form.

No "Kipping"

If you have half a brain, do not use the "kipping" technique that is often promoted by certain athletic trainers and displayed on some of their popular youtube.com video clips as a means to enhanced strength and fitness. When doing pull-ups and chin-ups, kipping is nothing more than an upper body version of plyometrics. When you "kip," it is your legs and momentum that are doing most of the work and not your arms, chest, shoulders, abs, and upper back muscles. Worse yet, the recoil effect at the bottom of the movement will eventually wreak havoc with your elbows and shoulders. Kipping is just a way to deceive yourself into thinking you're capable of doing reps that you cannot do. So be smart and use good form and muscular strength to achieve real and lasting results while protecting your joints, ligaments, and tendons. Remember, we are using this chinning exercise in its multiple variations to build lasting strength and to sculpt a perfectly muscled back. You won't have either one if you use your legs and cheat by using a kipping motion. So don't do it.

Conclusion

You may wish to completely "blow this chapter off" and look for an easier way to build your back. And truth to tell, you will have already achieved a much better than average back from the high volume push-up program that has already been presented, assuming that you have the guts and determination to follow it. But there is no better way to build a perfectly sculpted back in synergy with your biceps, forearms, and grip than incorporating this chinning program into your foundational training strategy two to three times each week. In fact, it will actually amplify your push-up gains, and nothing else will take its place or yield better results.

Granted, there will be some guys who try to come up with excuses for why they shouldn't focus their back program around chinning, such as "I weigh too much. My grip isn't strong enough. My arms are too long." If you want to talk yourself into believing that, it's up to you. But no way will you get the same results in terms of building your strength in direct proportion to your body weight with any other program.

The fact is, the pull-up is the best all-around back-building, arm-blasting exercise you can do in combination with the push-up. With pull-ups and push-ups, you hit every muscle in the entire body. And the pull-up hits the latissimus dorsi, teres major, posterior deltoid, rhomboids, the trapezius, biceps, triceps, chest, abs, and forearms—in other words, the pull-up in synergy with the push-up hits every muscle group in the entire upper body. There is nothing better or more complete.

Regardless of what specific chinning exercises you choose, the most important thing is you actually do them. *Often.* And don't ignore your back simply because you can't see it without using at least two carefully angled mirrors. It may not be as glamorous a body part as your biceps or chest, but your back is the one body part that will go the furthest in improving your overall strength, fitness, and physique for life.

BONUS chapter

power

Living Strength
24/7 Power Circuit
for Lifelong Strength & Fitness

"Simplicity is the ultimate sophistication."

Leonardo da Vinci

Living Strength 24/7 Power Circuit for Lifelong Strength & Fitness

John Peterson, *age 60,* May 2013.

After mastering *Ultimate Push-ups for the Awesome Physique,* you may wonder what's next? Truth to tell, if you have followed the program as outlined, you will be in great shape with an awesome physique by any normal standard, and you will now be ready to take on any fitness challenge you desire. That means you are now ready to practice any program you desire in the Living Strength Training System in order to achieve an even higher level of superior all-around health, strength, and athletic fitness for life. It also means that you are now ready for our *Living Strength 24/7 Power Circuit*—a workout comprised of four synergistic exercises that will get you in peak athletic condition and keep you there in just 24 minutes each day for as long as you do it, guaranteed!

Leonardo da Vinci had it right! Simplicity *is* the ultimate sophistication. With that in mind we want to encourage you to not let the *Living Strength 24/7 Power Workout's* simplicity and total lack of complication fool you. True strength, lifelong fitness, and a beautiful physique are not predicated on you performing an outrageous number of exercises or sets. Rather, it is the direct result of consuming the right nutrients and performing the right exercises at the right level of intensity. Think about that as you consider what you have read so far. Remember what you read in the history section? Woody Strode, Jock Mahoney, Robert Conrad, and Herschel Walker all had the same basic workout—push-ups, sit-ups and squats. A workout that if followed daily at the right level of intensity will yield extraordinary results. We have exactly the same workout outlined here plus one additional exercise for the biceps and upper body that will add the finishing touches to a perfect workout.

For the time invested—just 24 minutes of each day, 7 days each week—the *Living Strength Power Circuit* delivers the most thorough, measurable, comprehensive, and sustainable results of any program in the *history of natural health, strength, fitness, and bodybuilding!* And as you will quickly discover, it lays the perfect foundation for superior health, strength, and lifelong virility by combining the latest in exercise science from Dr. Laurence E. Morehouse with the same extraordinary methods of body-weight, self-resistance strength training that were taught by Charles Atlas and used by the ancient Grecian athletes of antiquity to build their bodies to "Greek god" perfection.

This course of four foundational exercises consists of 12 minutes of concentrated upper bodywork incorporated with 12 minutes of cardiovascular/pulmonary/lower body strength training for complete and synergistic total body fitness. All the guesswork is gone! This program has been *thoroughly tested* and is guaranteed to *produce superior results! But before beginning, it is imperative that you get a physical examination from your doctor and have his or her approval to start now!*

So let's cut to the chase. You're obviously not interested in delayed gratification. Neither is Rod or any of our friends who have tested this program. If you're like us, you don't have the luxury to sit around wasting time, and yet you want to *build and sculpt your muscles to perfection from head to toe* and do so as quickly as possible. But you wonder, *Is it really possible to accomplish that in just 24 minutes each day as Rod Fisher and John Peterson promise and with absolutely no special equipment required?* Answer: You bet it is, but it does require intense training. *You'll be training at high intensity with precision for 24 minutes straight with no rest.*

Bear in mind, Rod and I have promised you the best, simplest, and most effective bodybuilding and athletic fitness system—PERIOD. We never said that it would be easy. In fact, only an already superbly conditioned athlete will be able to complete this workout exactly as written the first few times he attempts it.

The Nuts and Bolts of the Program

Your "gym" will consist of a step, a towel, and a stopwatch (optional). All but perhaps the stopwatch can be found in any household. The reason for the stopwatch is that the exercises are timed (only in the beginning stages), so that you are motivated to get a certain high intensity *workload* accomplished within a *specified time period.* The reason for this is because it's not just how much exercise you do that builds muscles; *it's how much intensity you put into the actual contraction of the muscles* as they are working and the amount of nutrient rich, highly oxygenated blood that is delivered to them while they are working that *causes them to grow and adapt!*

Because this program has been created to deliver fantastic results in minimum time, you will be doing *only 4 exercises!* Three of them you already read about, because they come straight from the bios of Woody Strode, Robert Conrad, and Herschel Walker. They are the same exact exercises that many of us do first thing every morning. I have eliminated all but the most *ultra effective* exercises that deliver maximum results in minimum time. That means just *three dynamic exercises* that work your muscles synergistically in *groups.* I have forged these first three exercises into the *Living Strength 24/7 Power Circuit,* eliminating the need for rest periods.

What that means is this. While you are resting one group of muscles, you will be working another *unrelated* group, giving the first group time to *recuperate,* etc. Then, with your biceps, triceps, and forearms already pre-exhausted from the Power Circuit of three exercises, we have given you a fourth exercise that will not only work your biceps, triceps, and forearms, but will also strengthen, sculpt, and build every muscle in your entire upper body, including your abdominal muscles. Altogether, you will work up to exercising *24 minutes, nonstop with the 24/7 Power Circuit.*

Training in this fashion conserves time. While you are building your muscles, you will also be simultaneously giving your heart, lungs, and circulatory system a *terrific workout,* promoting superior health and *increasing both muscular strength and cardio endurance, while strectching and decompressing the spine all at the same time!* Now obviously, because of the intensity required, your body will be creating a great deal of heat, causing *fat-burning enzymes* to kick in, *burning off body fat* and bringing out *muscular definition* for that *ripped look that most men really want to achieve.* By extending yourself on each exercise, you will be *forcing your muscles to grow and adapt and ultimately become much stronger and more enduring as they take on that sculpted "Greek god" look.*

The way the Power Circuit is set up, you will start with the upper body (chest, shoulders, upper back, and arms), go to the mid section, and then work the hips, thighs, and calves, return to the midsection, back to the chest, shoulders, upper back, and arms, and finish up by *pumping the biceps, triceps, forearms, and entire upper body. Do not change any of the exercises or their sequence.* This is important! Move as quickly as possible while maintaining strict form.

Don't let any of the exercises intimidate you! Start at a number of reps that you can do without straining. For most of you having already performed the Ultimate Push-up Routine for at least one month you will be able to perform at least 30 Standard Military Push-ups, but if 20 reps is all you can do, you will still be building real strength, because bodybuilding/strength-building exercise is relative to a man's current physical condition. Try to add reps each week until you can perform the recommended number without undo fatigue. Then you can add other exercises from our other Living Strength body sculpting programs if you want to, or you can stay with *Living Strength 24/7 Power Circuit* for the rest of your life, knowing that you already have everything necessary to stay in perfect shape for life.

The Living Strength Power Circuit Difference

Over the years, I have known many men who have tried just about every bodybuilding system known to man. These systems were guaranteed to add pounds and pounds of muscle to their frames in world-record time. Virtually all of them were based on the use of heavy weights. A good example of the kind of training

I'm talking about was Peary Rader's Breathing Squat Program. With that program a trainee was advised to load a barbell up to the maximum amount of weight that he could squat for 10 consecutive repetitions and then force himself to complete 20 consecutive repetitions with that same weight. Naturally, if one survived and didn't get injured right away following such a program, he did gain a great deal of weight because he was also encouraged to eat a great deal. In fact, that program and variations of it virtually guaranteed gigantic thighs, a huge butt, a big gut, and a severely compressed lower spine. It was the perfect routine for achieving what some might call a "bridge troll look." All in all, most of the men whom I have known who followed such programs long term ended up with *the wrong kind of gain and all kinds of pain.* Not exactly something you want if you have half a brain.

I tell you this for one reason. It's because that is not the kind of result you will achieve from following this or any program from the Living Strength Training System. You will not add pounds and pounds of useless weight on your thighs, butt, and gut. You will add perfectly sculpted muscle mass to be sure. But it will be in all the right places with emphasis on arms, chest, shoulders, and upper back while slimming and sculpting the waistline for a very obvious "V" shaped look. You will also strengthen your heart and expand your lung capacity to achieve high level strength and athleticism while simultaneously losing extraneous body fat. In other words, all the good stuff will happen and none of the bad.

Here's the big payoff. For the results obtained in the time spent, nobody is going to improve on the *Living Strength 24/7 Power Circuit!* We have created this comprehensive, yet thoroughly efficient course to work the major muscle groups of the body *intensely and with the utmost efficiency,* meaning the shortest possible time. The muscles are worked synergistically in groups, as opposed to isolating each muscle. Plus, these groups are pumped thoroughly on the first set, eliminating the need for a huge number of exercises or numerous sets! Worked this way, the muscles unite to coordinate their exertion, making them much stronger and more efficient than if they were worked separately. The physique then takes on a more natural, graceful look like that of Charles Atlas or the ancient Grecian athletes as the muscle groups blend in with one another.

The circuit itself takes only 20 minutes, and all the major muscle groups are developed along with the cardiovascular/pulmonary systems. Then, after the muscles have already been pre-exhausted, we have added 4 minutes of bicep/upper bodywork, which is not absolutely necessary, as the circuit builds thick, powerful arms, along with the rest of the body. However, throughout history, shapely, muscular biceps have been the trademark of the "Greek god," "he-man" physique, and your arms are often more visible than the rest of your body, so we added this as a bonus exercise, bringing the entire course up to 24 minutes!

Why I Developed the Living Strength 24/7 Power Circuit

Throughout the years, I have observed firsthand that all of the bodybuilding and fitness courses that were popularly promoted in magazines were too time-consuming, too incomplete, or required special equipment that was not readily available for the busy man to incorporate into his lifestyle. Not only did most courses waste time with the rest periods between exercises and sets of exercises, they did not include cardiovascular exercise. You would still have to jog, run, cycle, or swim, etc., in addition to performing your bodybuilding exercises, if you wanted to achieve total strength, fitness, and dynamic health! For this reason I decided to eliminate the rest periods and integrate the cardiovascular work right into the muscle building!

By studying the foundational training methods taught by the giants of the Golden Age of Physical Culture, including such men as Alois P. Swoboda, Bernarr Macfadden, Edwin Checkley, and Charles Atlas, it became obvious that it does not take countless sets or dozens of exercises to acquire an impressive body as long as there are a few foundational exercises that are part of every day's training. And it was further substantiated when I read the training programs of Woody Strode, Jock Mahoney, Robert Conrad, Herschel Walker, Antonino Rocca, and others. Thus, a few correctly chosen exercises, performed for just a couple of intense sets, will accomplish the results of many. After many years of testing a wide number of possibilities and much trial and error, the *Living Strength 24/7 Power Circuit* was born.

Here are the exercises presented in circuit sequence. As you can see, there are no wasted moves—no wasted time!

EXERCISE ONE

Living Strength Push-up

(or any variation you choose)

NOTE: Although the *Living Strength 24/7 Power Circuit* is based on using the Standard Military Push-up as the foundational upper-body strength building exercise, advanced men are welcome to use any variation they choose. In fact, extremely advanced men may choose the Living Strength variation pictured above.

If this is your choice, bear in mind that you will be moving 85% of your body weight with each repetition as opposed to 55% with the Standard Military Push-up.

Using simple math, this means that if you are a 200-pound man performing 50 Living Strength Push-ups in each set, you will be moving 170 pounds x 50 repetitions, which equals 8,500 pounds moved through an extended range in just one minute. In effect, this is an upper-body sprint simultaneously building heart, lungs, arms, chest, shoulders, upper back, lower back, abs, hips, and upper and lower legs. No other exercise accomplishes so much so quickly.

EXERCISE TWO & FOUR

Full Range Atlas Sit-up

(or its alternate)

Do this exercise properly, and you will have a flat, perfectly sculpted, and muscular waistline regardless of your age. (I'm 60 and my waistline measures just 29".) It will also reward you with dramatically enhanced athleticism and a super charged libido. In addition, you will have a supple, flexible, and pain-free lower spine with built-in protection against hernia. Better still, performed in this sequence, you will be eliminating the need for additional waist work. *The key* is to not have anyone hold your feet down and allow muscular tension alone to do the job. By doing so, your lower abdominal muscles will be thoroughly worked Isometrically while your upper abs are being exercised Isotonically, resulting in a fantastically effective ab-sculpting exercise.

Starting position: Lie flat on your back, legs straight, back of heels flat on the floor with heels close together and hands clasped behind head.

Action: "Curl" your upper body upward and forward toward your legs until your elbows touch your thighs. In time, as your flexibility improves, you may try to touch your forehead to your knees, and eventually you may even be able to touch your chin to your knees, as was recommended by Charles Atlas in the original Charles Atlas Course that was written in 1922 (the foundation upon which we built the Living Strength Training system).

Your goal is 2 sets of 75 to 100 consecutive reps performed in a circuit as instructed.

ALTERNATE

Atlas Sit-up II

(the alternate to the Full Range Atlas)

If the Atlas Sit-Up I causes too much discomfort, you should perform this alternate. Like the Atlas I, if you do this exercise properly, you *will* have a flat chiseled waistline along with a supple and flexible lower spine and built in protection against hernia. Once again, the key is to not have anyone or anything holding or pinning your feet down. By doing so, your lower abdominal muscles will be exercised intensely through Isometric Contraction while your upper abs are being exercised Isotonically, resulting in a fantastically effective ab-sculpting exercise.

Starting position: Lie flat on your back with hands clasped behind your head. Knees bent and heels as close to your buttocks as possible.

Action: Curl your upper body toward your legs until your elbows touch your thighs. Lower and repeat.

The goal is 2 sets of 75 to 100 reps.

The Key to the entire *Living Strength Power Circuit* and creating a *ripped physique* is daily performance of either of the two following exercises.

EXERCISE THREE

Living Strength Power Step-up

(or its alternate)

Special Note: *If for some reason, previous injury to your knees or hips prevents you from performing the Tiger Bend Squat then substitute the Living Strength Power Step-up. It works the same muscles from a different perspective. You can also alternate daily and perform the Tiger Bend Squat on one day and the Living Strength Power Step-up the next. The important thing is to achieve a level of strength, flexibility, and endurance that allows you to achieve 12 consecutive minutes of intense muscular effort nonstop.*

Use a regular stair step or stool over 7" *but not over* 12" high. Step up with left foot, then right foot, down with left foot, then with right foot. This is 1 step. Your goal is to aim for 42 reps per minute. This exercise is recognized as a full-fledged cardio-aerobic exercise by the National Aerobics Institute founded by Dr. Kenneth Cooper. It conditions the cardiovascular system, while at the same time promoting enhanced lung capacity and improved full body circulation and endurance. The 12 minutes is a must for a trim, athletic physique, as it builds, sculpts, and strengthens the hips, glutes, thighs, and calves. And just as the Tiger Bend Squat sends your metabolism into hyperdrive, so will the Living Strength Power Step-up. At 12 minutes, your body will kick in with a fat-burning enzyme that will assure you of a trim, muscular physique. About every 42 steps, lead off with the opposite foot to equalize benefits.

All in all, your goal is to perform 500 step-ups in 12 minutes.

ALTERNATE

Tiger Bend Squat

(the alternate to the Power Step-up)

When properly performed, no exercise delivers as much full range strength, flexibility, and endurance (both muscular and cardio) as does the Tiger Bend Squat. Not only that, but due to the amount of muscle mass that it builds, sculpts, and develops, it will also eliminate excess fat from your hips, glutes, and waistline (front, sides, and back) in world-record time as it sends your metabolism into hyperdrive.

But here's the deal. Your goal is to ultimately work up to 300 to 360 consecutive repetitions in 12 minutes. When you accomplish this, you will be awed by your newly developed leg strength, sense of balance, and enhanced lung capacity as your body takes on a feeling of being incredibly strong, lithe, flexible, and light. In fact, when you get to the point where you can accomplish the entire circuit in 24 minutes in good form, your strength, fitness, and physique will be off the charts compared to all but the most elite athletes.

Starting position: (Photo 1) Feet shoulder-width apart. Toes are pointing straight ahead. Hands in tight fists at chest level. (Photo 2) While keeping your back straight, hands reaching and extending your arms down and behind you, bend your knees and descend to the bottom position. (Photo 3) Your arms are swinging forward while you are descending and you should simultaneously be raising your heels

from the floor until you reach the bottom position at which time your arms will be in a straight line down from your shoulders and your fingers brush the floor. (Photo 4) Now continue swinging your arms forward and upward while pushing off from your toes and raising your body to a standing position. (This is great for enhancing your sense of balance.) (Photo 5) At this point your arms have continued to move forward and upward until they are in a straight line in front of you from your shoulders. (Photo 6) At this point your hands are now in tight fists and you will draw them back to the original starting position next to your sides at chest level. Inhale as you pull them in and exhale as you lower your body.

Repeat as smoothly and steadily as you can. Once you begin you'll notice that the arms take on a smooth, rhythmic motion not unlike rowing a boat. The movement, steps 1 through 6, is one continuous, smooth movement. 30 repetitions is a great start. 100 without stopping is excellent, and once you are completing 300 to 360 in 12 minutes, you will have extraordinary strength, endurance, flexibility, coordination, balance, speed, and your lower body will have a beautifully balanced musculature. And after you have achieved this level for a period of 2 to 3 months you will notice that you can knock off a thousand repetitions whenever you feel like it.

EXERCISE SIX

The Milo

(for awesome arms)

Biceps need to be worked synergistically with triceps and forearms for balanced full arm development. To hit the biceps with great intensity as well as triceps, forearms, chest, shoulders, upper back, and abs (yes, it does all that), I use "The Milo." And by the way, to not fully engage the forearms by clenching your fists as tightly as possible when performing biceps contractions is to diminish the effectiveness of the exercise.

Starting position: Stand erect with your feet about 12" apart. Clench both fists as tightly as possible in a "hammerfist" (as shown) and place them with your left fist over your right fist just below your waistline at about 6" from the centerline of your body. With your right arm pulling up and your left arm pressing down with great resistance, slowly pull your right arm up until both fists are in front of your face. Then reverse the movement, pressing your left arm down against resistance provided by the right arm. Continue for 20 consecutive repetitions and then switch arms with right fist over left. Continue for another 20 repetitions. Then switch arms and continue for an additional 15 reps on each side. At that point you are finished. Congratulations.

The Living Strength 24/7 Power Circuits are designed to deliver maximum results in minimum time. Each Power Circuit workout strongly emphasizes complete arm, chest, shoulder, and upper back development, while also creating a ripped waistline, slim musclular hips, and power packed thighs.

Gregory Rohm, age 36 (pictured here with his daughter), is a perfect example of the results that can be achieved by consistent application of the 24/7 Power Circuit. His current record for Level 3 is 35:19.

LEVEL 1 24/7 POWER CIRCUIT

EXERCISE	REPETITIONS	TIME ALLOTMENT
MILITARY PUSH-UPS	40-50	1 MINUTE
ATLAS SIT-UPS	75	3 MINUTES
TIGER BEND SQUATS	300	12 MINUTES
ATLAS SIT-UPS	75	3 MINUTES
MILITARY PUSH-UPS	40-50	1 MINUTE
THE MILO (OPTIONAL)	20 & 15 (EACH ARM)	4 MINUTES
	TOTAL TIME REQUIRED:	24 MINUTES

For Advanced Body Sculpting & Conditioning

After practicing the *Living Strength 24/7 Power Circuit* as your foundational strength and fitness program for some months, you may decide that you want to step it up further in order to achieve an extraordinary level of functional strength and fitness for athletic pursuits or to further enhance and perfect your physique. If that's the case, Rod and I recommend the following modifications to the program. Doing so will add only five minutes each day to your workout, but you will be awed by the added intensity and results.

LEVEL 2 24/7 POWER CIRCUIT

EXERCISE	REPETITIONS	TIME ALLOTMENT
MILITARY PUSH-UPS	40-50	1 MINUTE
ATLAS SIT-UPS	75	3 MINUTES
TIGER BEND SQUATS	100	4 MINUTES
MILITARY PUSH-UPS	40-50	1 MINUTE
ATLAS SIT-UPS	75	3 MINUTES
TIGER BEND SQUATS	100	4 MINUTES
MILITARY PUSH-UPS	40-50	1 MINUTE
ATLAS SIT-UPS	75	3 MINUTES
TIGER BEND SQUATS	100	4 MINUTES
MILITARY PUSH-UPS	40-50	1 MINUTE
THE MILO (OPTIONAL)	20 & 15 (EACH ARM)	4 MINUTES
	TOTAL TIME REQUIRED:	29 MINUTES

For Extreme Strength, Conditioning & Body Sculpting

If you're a competitive boxer, wrestler, a practitioner of mixed martial arts, a rock climber, a physical culturist, or a man who thrives on self-mastery and challenge, you will want to have a competitive edge 24/7, and the *Living Strength 24/7 Power Circuit* will give you that edge and keep it there. Only a man in extraordinary condition will be able to complete this circuit in the time alotted on a consistent basis. Yet, even at this level, LSF III does not require more than 40 minutes total, and that is assuming that you are taking reasonable rest periods between exercises when absolutely necessary.

LEVEL 3 24/7 POWER CIRCUIT

EXERCISE	REPETITIONS	TIME ALLOTMENT
MILITARY PUSH-UPS	50	1 MINUTE
ATLAS SIT-UPS	75	3 MINUTES
TIGER BEND SQUATS	100	4 MINUTES
MILITARY PUSH-UPS	50	1 MINUTE
ATLAS SIT-UPS	75	3 MINUTES
TIGER BEND SQUATS	100	4 MINUTES
MILITARY PUSH-UPS	50	1 MINUTE
ATLAS SIT-UPS	75	3 MINUTES
TIGER BEND SQUATS	100	4 MINUTES
MILITARY PUSH-UPS	50	1 MINUTE
ATLAS SIT-UPS	75	3 MINUTES
TIGER BEND SQUATS	100	4 MINUTES
THE MILO (OPTIONAL)	20 & 15 (EACH ARM)	4 MINUTES
	TOTAL TIME REQUIRED:	36 MINUTES

In addition to the *Living Strength Training Circuits* outlined above, Rod and I invite you to purchase our other books and courses that teach you how to achieve and maintain Super Health, Strength, Fitness & Healing for Life!

WEEK: **1**

LIVING STRENGTH™ DAILY PUSH-UPS

	MON	TUE	WED	THU	FRI	SAT	SUN
%	35%	50%	60%	30%	50%	40%	25%
6AM							
7AM							
8AM							
9AM							
10AM							
11AM							
12PM							
1PM							
2PM							
3PM							
4PM							
5PM							
6PM							
7PM							
8PM							
9PM							
10PM							
TOTAL							

LIVING STRENGTH™

DAILY PUSH-UPS

	MON	TUE	WED	THU	FRI	SAT	SUN
%	40%	65%	35%	70%	40%	50%	30%
6AM							
7AM							
8AM							
9AM							
10AM							
11AM							
12PM							
1PM							
2PM							
3PM							
4PM							
5PM							
6PM							
7PM							
8PM							
9PM							
10PM							
TOTAL							

WEEK: **3**

LIVING STRENGTH™

DAILY PUSH-UPS

	MON	TUE	WED	THU	FRI	SAT	SUN
%	40%	50%	75%	45%	80%	60%	25%
6AM							
7AM							
8AM							
9AM							
10AM							
11AM							
12PM							
1PM							
2PM							
3PM							
4PM							
5PM							
6PM							
7PM							
8PM							
9PM							
10PM							
TOTAL							

WEEK: **4**

LIVING STRENGTH™

DAILY PUSH-UPS

	MON	TUE	WED	THU	FRI	SAT	SUN
%	90%	45%	25%	65%	80%	35%	20%
6AM							
7AM							
8AM							
9AM							
10AM							
11AM							
12PM							
1PM							
2PM							
3PM							
4PM							
5PM							
6PM							
7PM							
8PM							
9PM							
10PM							
TOTAL							

WEEK:

LIVING STRENGTH™

DAILY PUSH-UPS

	MON	TUE	WED	THU	FRI	SAT	SUN
%							
6AM							
7AM							
8AM							
9AM							
10AM							
11AM							
12PM							
1PM							
2PM							
3PM							
4PM							
5PM							
6PM							
7PM							
8PM							
9PM							
10PM							
TOTAL							